IMAGES
of Rail

NORTHWESTERN PENNSYLVANIA RAILROADS

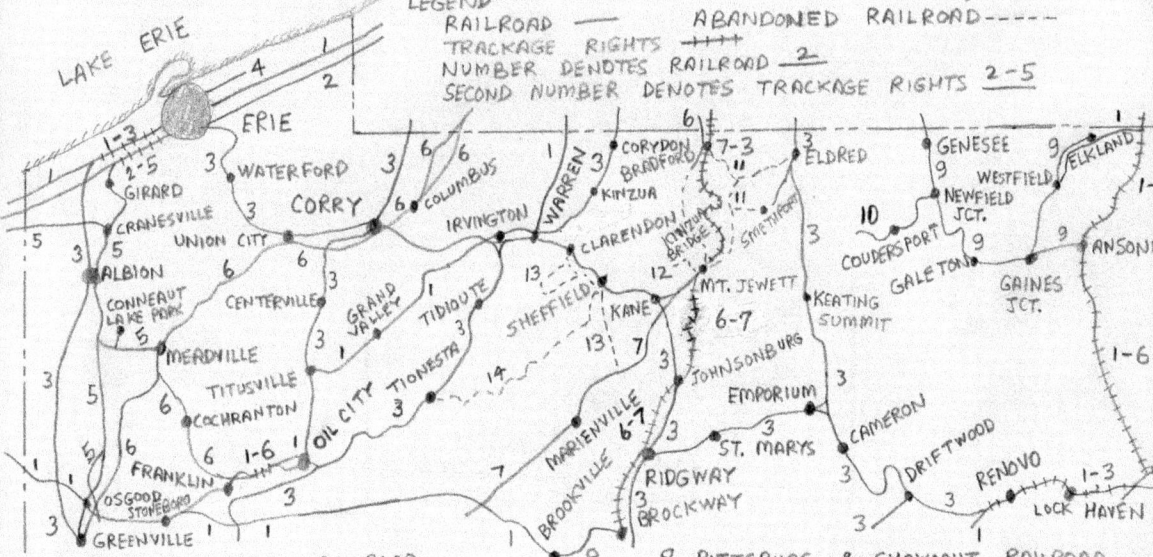

NORTH WESTERN PENNSYLVANIA RAILROAD MAP
JUNE 30, 1960

LEGEND
RAILROAD ————— ABANDONED RAILROAD - - - - -
TRACKAGE RIGHTS ++++++
NUMBER DENOTES RAILROAD 2
SECOND NUMBER DENOTES TRACKAGE RIGHTS 2-5

1 NEW YORK CENTRAL RAILROAD
2 NEW YORK CHICAGO & ST. LOUIS RAILROAD (NICKEL PLATE)
3 PENNSYLVANIA RAILROAD
4 EAST ERIE COMMERCIAL RAILROAD
5 BESSEMER & LAKE ERIE RAILROAD
6 ERIE RAILROAD
7 BALTIMORE & OHIO RAILROAD
8 PITTSBURG & SHAWMUT RAILROAD
9 WELLSVILLE, ADDISON & GALETON RAILROAD
10 COUDERSPORT & PORT ALLEGANY RAILROAD
11 BRADFORD, BORDELL & KINZUA RAILROAD
12 MT. JEWETT, KINZUA & RITERVILLE RAILROAD
13 TIONESTA VALLEY RAILWAY
14 SHEFFIELD & TIONESTA RAILWAY

This is a June 30, 1960, map of railroads in northwestern Pennsylvania. Many of these lines have been abandoned, including Pennsylvania Railroad lines from Titusville via Corry to Brocton, New York; Oil City via Tidioute to Irvineton; and Warren via Corydon into New York State.

IMAGES
of Rail

NORTHWESTERN
PENNSYLVANIA
RAILROADS

Kenneth C. Springirth

ARCADIA
PUBLISHING

Published by Arcadia Publishing
Charleston, South Carolina

Library of Congress Control Number: 2010921769

For all general information contact Arcadia Publishing at:
Telephone 843-853-2070
Fax 843-853-0044
E-mail sales@arcadiapublishing.com
For customer service and orders:
Toll-Free 1-888-313-2665

Visit us on the Internet at www.arcadiapublishing.com

This book is dedicated to the author's granddaughter Elisabeth Elliot Springirth who in this February 15, 2010, scene is very observant and is developing a keen interest in books. (Photograph by Peter A. Springirth.)

CONTENTS

ACKNOWLEDGMENTS

Thanks to the members of the Lake Shore Railway Historical Society, Inc., for saving, preserving, and establishing a public museum with a number of vintage railroad cars and locomotives on display at the former Lake Shore and Michigan Southern Railway passenger station at Robinson and Wall Streets in North East, Pennsylvania. Raymond E. Grabowski, president of the Lake Shore Railway Historical Society, Inc., which operates the Lake Shore Railway Museum (mailing address P.O. Box 571, North East, Pennsylvania 16428-0571 and telephone number 814-725-1911), was very helpful with providing information and allowed me to look at back issues of their newsletter, *The Lake Shore Timetable*. Gerald N. D'Aurora was a source for photographs and information. The Kane Historic Preservation Society (P.O. Box 525, Kane, Pennsylvania 16735) board members, Dennis Driscoll, John Marconi, Scott Morgan, and Richard Bly, provided pictures and information. Dennis Sturdevant, president of the Sheffield Depot Preservation Society, Inc. (75 Center Street, P.O. Box 671, Sheffield, Pennsylvania 16347), provided pictures and information. Dennis Mead, president of the French Creek Valley Railroad Historical Society (P.O. Box 632 Meadville, Pennsylvania 16335, Web site: www.fcvrrhs.org), provided information on railroads in Crawford County. Jim Nelson, president of the Corry Historical Society, provided information on the Erie Railroad train station in Corry. Jim Mason, president of the Lawrence Park Historical Society, provided pictures. Donald Kaverman provided pictures and reference information. Herbert Wildman provided information. The Heritage Room of the Blasco Memorial Library of the Erie County Public Library maintained old newspapers on microfilm making it possible to find a wealth of information in the following newspapers: *Erie Morning Dispatch*, *Erie Sunday Dispatch*, *Erie Gazette*, *Erie Daily Times*, and *Erie Morning News*. Information was found in issues of the *Corry Journal* and the *Titusville Herald*. Research was also done at the Iroquois Avenue Branch and Millcreek Branch of the Erie County Public Library system, plus the Albion Public Library in Albion and the Benson Memorial Library in Titusville. Reference books June 1916 *Official Guide of the Railways* and August 1936 *Official Guide of the Railways*, *History of Erie County, Pennsylvania Volume I* by John Elmer Reed, *A Twentieth Century History of Erie County Volume I* by John Miller, and *Kane and the Upper Allegheny* by J. E. Henretta provided background information. Unless otherwise noted, all images appear courtesy of the author.

INTRODUCTION

An agreement was reached November 17, 1853, to establish a uniform gauge from Buffalo to Cleveland. Work to change the gauge began December 7, 1853, but that evening a large group of Erie citizens tore down the railroad bridges over State and French Streets. Farmers tore up track in Harborcreek. During the time period that the citizens prevented the unified track gauge, passengers and freight were transferred between Harborcreek and Erie by stages and horses. The gauge change was completed February 1, 1854. In 1864, Union Depot replaced the first passenger train station. During 1869, railroads between Chicago and Buffalo were combined into the Lake Shore and Michigan Southern Railway. By August 1871, the Dunkirk, Warren, and Pittsburgh Railroad completed their line from Dunkirk, New York, to connect with the Philadelphia and Erie Railroad at Warren. Passenger service began on June 22, 1871, from Dunkirk to Falconer, New York. On December 31, 1872, it merged with the Warren and Venango Railroad to form the Dunkirk, Allegheny Valley, and Pittsburgh Railroad, which was leased to the New York Central and Hudson River Railroad on January 3, 1873. A speed record was set on October 24, 1895, when a Chicago to Buffalo train made the 510.1-mile run in 481 minutes and 7 seconds at an average speed of 65.7 miles per hour. At two locations between Buffalo and Erie, the train reached a speed of 96 miles per hour.

The passenger train *Twentieth Century Limited* began service in 1902, making the 960-mile trip from New York to Chicago in 20 hours at an average speed of 80 miles per hour. In 1914, the New York Central and Hudson River Railroad and the Lake Shore and Michigan Southern Railway were combined to form the New York Central Railroad. By 1935, travel time for the *Twentieth Century Limited* was reduced to 16.5 hours. Passenger service from Dunkirk, New York, to Titusville, Pennsylvania, ended June 13, 1937. After World War II, there was a significant decline in passenger and freight revenues. The completion of the New York Thruway and St. Lawrence Seaway contributed to a continued decline in railroad revenues. The New York Central Railroad line from Titusville to Warren was abandoned during 1966 except for the 2.5-mile Fieldmore Springs line between Titusville and East Titusville. Following the February 1, 1968, merger of the New York Central Railroad and Pennsylvania Railroad into the Penn Central Transportation Company, financial losses continued, and bankruptcy was declared on June 21, 1970. Under the Railroad Revitalization and Regulatory Reform Act, Consolidated Rail Corporation was formed. Hurricane Agnes washed out a bridge just west of Sinclairville, New York, in 1972 resulting in the abandonment of the line from Fredonia to Falconer, New York. The line from Falconer, New York, to Warren, Pennsylvania, was abandoned with the formation of Consolidated Rail Corporation on April 1, 1976.

Chartered in 1856, by 1864 the Erie and Pittsburgh Railroad was completed from Erie to New Castle. On March 1, 1870, it was leased to the Pennsylvania Railroad for 999 years. Groundbreaking for the Sunbury and Erie Railroad was June 3, 1851, near Farrandsville, Clinton County, about 7 miles from Lock Haven. The first section of what became the Philadelphia and Erie Railroad was completed from Milton to Williamsport on December 18, 1854, followed by Milton to Sunbury on January 7, 1856. Passenger train service on the Philadelphia to Erie line of what later became the Pennsylvania Railroad began on October 5, 1864, with a special excursion. The *Erie Dispatch* newspaper for October 6, 1864, declared, "All hail to the iron band which now joins Erie with Philadelphia and the seaboard." Regular passenger service began October 17, 1864, over the entire line and ended on March 27, 1965, when train No. 580 left Erie at 5:45 p.m. with extra cars for the crowd making the last eastbound trip. In 1982, Consolidated Rail Corporation abandoned the line from Erie to Irvine but kept the section open from Corry to Union City. The *Corry Journal* newspaper of January 9, 1984, reported that the line between Corry and Union City was shut down, noting, "The last empty car from Union City was brought back to Corry over the weekend." In the May 6, 1985, the *Corry Journal* newspaper announced that Hammermill Paper Company would purchase the former Pennsylvania Railroad main line from Erie to Emporium. The November 10, 1985, *Erie Times News* newspaper reported, "The railroad tracks between Erie and Emporium, now owned by Hammermill Paper Company's Allegheny Railroad Company, are still under repair, but the railroad's vice president (H. LeRoy Weidner) said the track should be ready for 40 mph trains by the end of 1986 and the Allegheny Railroad is in business to stay." It was used to ship product between Hammermill Paper Company plants in Lock Haven and Erie. On October 31, 1992, the Allegheny and Eastern Railroad, a subsidiary of Genesee and Wyoming, Inc., purchased the railroad, which was merged into the Buffalo and Pittsburgh Railroad, another subsidiary of Genesee and Wyoming, Inc., on January 1, 2004. The main line of the Buffalo and Pittsburgh Railroad is from Buffalo, New York, via Salamanca, New York, to Eidenau, Pennsylvania (north of Pittsburgh), with branch lines to Erie, Driftwood, and Indiana.

Following the discovery of oil on August 27, 1859, just south of Titusville with the first well that produced oil in abundance drilled by William A. Smith under the supervision of Edwin L. Drake, the new petroleum industry began and within a day the rush was on to buy land and drill a well. Transporting oil to market was difficult. Oil was loaded on flatboats and floated downstream on Oil Creek and the Allegheny River to Pittsburgh. However, in the summer when water levels were low, oil was hauled overland to the nearest railroad station about 25 miles north of Titusville at Corry, Union City, or Garland. Oil leaking from barrels on the horse-drawn wagons mixed with the muddy road creating a gooey paste. At times, wagons dropped into mud holes below their axles. All of this changed when the first railroad to reach Pennsylvania's oil region, the Oil Creek Railroad, chartered August 17, 1860, completed their line from Corry to Miller Farm in 1862 and reached Petroleum Centre in 1866. At Corry, connections were made with the Philadelphia and Erie Railroad and the Atlantic and Great Western Railroad.

The Farmers Railroad completed their line from Oil City to Petroleum Centre in 1867. By 1868, the Farmers Railroad and the Oil Creek Railroad merged to form the Oil Creek and Allegheny River Railway, which, during 1870, constructed a railroad on the east bank of Oil Creek between Petroleum Centre and Titusville under the name Titusville and Petroleum Centre Railroad. Both lines were used until the west line was abandoned during 1933. On July 12, 1885, the Buffalo and Oil Creek Cross Cut Railroad was organized in the state of New York to build a railroad line from Brocton, New York, to Corry, Pennsylvania. It merged with the Cross Cut Railroad (organized in Pennsylvania) on October 18, 1867, to become the Buffalo, Corry, and Pittsburg Railway and later Western New York and Pennsylvania Railroad that came under control of the Pennsylvania Railroad on July 31, 1900. General, freight, and petroleum products moved over this line from Pittsburgh to Buffalo.

In 1916, the Pennsylvania Railroad began using the slogan "Standard Railroad of the World" with the objective of being thought of as the standard to which all other railroads aspired, and this was true for many years. This was the first railroad to completely replace wooden-bodied passenger cars with steel-bodied cars and the first to develop baggage tags for passenger luggage. Through passenger service from Pittsburgh via Titusville to Buffalo ended in 1949. The last Pennsylvania Railroad passenger train through Titusville was train No. 980 from Oil City to Corry on June 9, 1953. The Pennsylvania Railroad merged into the New York Central Railroad, forming Penn

Central Transportation Company on February 1, 1968, which merged into Consolidated Rail Corporation on April 1, 1976. Trackage from Titusville north was abandoned with the last train operated from Corry to Brocton on December 29, 1978. The last train operated to Titusville and East Titusville on August 17, 1981. On February 5, 1984, Consolidated Rail Corporation abandoned the line from Rynd Farm to Titusville.

Encountering difficulty in obtaining terms for its franchise through Erie, workers of the Nickel Plate Road laid out ties and rails in the early morning of Sunday, April 2, 1882, and before evening, the line was completed to run a train. This eliminated the delay that would have occurred during a weekday when a civil process might have halted the work. Its first through passenger train reached Erie from the west on August 31, 1882, and regular passenger service began October 23, 1882. During World War II, the Nickel Plate Road became a highly efficient railroad offering the shortest and fastest route between Chicago and Buffalo. On May 13, 1949, the railroad received its last new steam locomotive, Berkshire No. 779, which was also the last steam locomotive built by the Lima Locomotive Works. There were 80 Berkshire steam locomotives on the Nickel Plate Road gaining fame due to their fine performance, efficient design, and handsome appearance. The railroad retired its last steam engines on August 1, 1960, and became officially dieselized. Effective October 16, 1964, the Nickel Plate Road merged into the Norfolk and Western Railway. The former Nickel Plate Road's last passenger trains, *City of Chicago* and *City of Cleveland*, were discontinued on September 9, 1965. On December 31, 1990, the Norfolk and Western Railway and Southern Railway became the Norfolk Southern Railway.

Over the years, the Erie Railroad operated three daily trains in each direction from New York via Meadville to Chicago offering good service with sleeping cars, diners, and deluxe coaches. The Erie Railroad and the Delaware, Lackawanna, and Western Railroad merged into the Erie-Lackawanna Railroad on October 17, 1960, and upgraded their large car repair shop in Meadville. On June 18, 1963, William White became chairman of the board and chief executive officer and the hyphen was removed, making it Erie Lackawanna Railroad. On April 1, 1968, it became Erie Lackawanna Railway, formed as a subsidiary of Dereco, the holding company of the Norfolk and Western Railway. In 1972, Hurricane Agnes destroyed much of the railroad's track, and the company filed for bankruptcy on June 26, 1972. It was merged into the Consolidated Rail Corporation on April 1, 1976.

The final railroad reaching Erie was the Pittsburg, Shenango, and Lake Erie Railroad, which began passenger service into Erie in June 1892. This became the Bessemer and Lake Erie Railroad on December 31, 1900.

The New York, Lake Erie, and Western Railroad had engineer Octave Chanute design the Kinzua Bridge and the Phoenix Iron Works build it; the bridge was originally constructed from wrought iron and completed on August 29, 1882. For two years, this bridge held the record as the tallest railroad bridge in the world. In 1893, the New York, Lake Erie, and Western Railroad went bankrupt and on November 6, 1895, became the Erie Railroad, which became the bridge owner. With heavier locomotives, the bridge could no longer safely carry trains, and the last train crossed the bridge on May 14, 1900. Construction of the new steel bridge, designed by C. R. Grimm to accommodate heavier trains, began on May 26, 1900, by the Elmira Bridge Company using the original (1882) masonry pedestals. The bridge was reopened to traffic on September 25, 1900. After the Erie Railroad obtained trackage rights on the nearby Baltimore and Ohio Railroad to bypass the aging bridge, train service over the bridge ended on June 21, 1959. The Erie Railroad sold the bridge to the Kovalchick Salvage Company. On August 12, 1963, Pennsylvania governor William Scranton signed a bill to purchase the bridge and nearby land to create Kinzua Bridge State Park, which opened in 1970.

The Knox and Kane Railroad operated a 97-mile round-trip excursion from Marienville via Kane and over the Kinzua Bridge. The bridge was closed in 2002 to recreational pedestrian and railroad usage after engineers determined the structure was at risk to high winds, but the railroad continued to operate excursion trains to the bridge's western approach. Work began in February 2003 to restore the bridge. Following the July 21, 2003, tornado that destroyed most of the Kinzua Bridge, the state decided not to rebuild it. It would have cost an estimated $45 million. In addition, there was a serious decline in freight business plus deterioration of the trackage, which resulted in the end of freight service in the spring of 2006. The locomotives were severely damaged by fire on March 16, 2008. On October 10–11, 2008, the rolling stock of the Knox and Kane Railroad was auctioned off as part of a liquidation sale. The railroad filed for abandonment.

The Brookville and Mahoning Railroad (later called Pittsburg and Shawmut Railroad) was planned to connect with the Pittsburgh area by the parent company, the Pittsburg, Shawmut, and Northern Railroad. By 1916, the Pittsburg and Shawmut Railroad separated from the parent company. While the Pittsburg, Shawmut, and Northern Railroad had financial difficulties and made its last run on April 1, 1947, the Pittsburg and Shawmut Railroad eventually prospered. The 88-mile main line of the railroad was from Brockway via Brookville and Kittanning to Freeport. With a decline in coal traffic on April 27, 1996, the railroad was sold to Genesee and Wyoming, Inc. On January 2, 1900, the Sheffield and Tionesta Railroad was incorporated to build a 24-mile line from Sheffield to Kellettville. By 1911, the line opened to Tionesta. The railroad ended service September 17, 1943.

In 1932, the Buffalo and Susquehanna Railroad was merged into the Baltimore and Ohio Railroad. This included the 37-mile line built in 1895 from Wellsville, New York, to Galeton, Pennsylvania; the 54-mile line from Addison, New York, to Galeton, Pennsylvania; and the 8-mile line from Galeton to Ansonia. These lines were purchased by the Wellsville, Addison, and Galeton Railroad, which was incorporated in 1954 and began operation on January 1, 1956.

With the closure of the Sinclair Oil Refinery in Wellsville, the railroad suffered a major loss in business and purchased a number of freight cars, which were placed into interchange service to augment revenues. When structural weakness was noted on a bridge between Elkland and Addison, the Interstate Commerce Commission approved the abandonment of that section, which also did not have any freight customers, and the track was removed in 1960. The Wellsville, Addison, and Galeton Railroad purchased the 16-mile Coudersport and Port Allegany Railroad in 1964, but the Interstate Commerce Commission approved this line, along with the Wellsville branch, for abandonment in May 1970. Flooding, and loss of business from the flooding, resulted in the Interstate Commerce Commission approving the abandonment of the remaining Wellsville, Addison, and Galeton Railroad trackage with the final freight run made on March 13, 1979, and the final movement of locomotives to various buyers on November 7, 1979.

The Rochester and State Line Railroad completed a line from Rochester to Salamanca, New York, in 1878 and became the Rochester and Pittsburgh Railroad in 1881. On March 10, 1887, it was consolidated into the Buffalo, Rochester, and Pittsburgh Railway. It reached into the coalfields of Pennsylvania and was purchased by the Baltimore and Ohio Railroad on January 1, 1932. Since 1988, many of its lines in Pennsylvania have been operated by the Buffalo and Pittsburgh Railroad.

The Oil Creek and Titusville Railroad began passenger excursion service on July 18, 1986, using diesel locomotive No. 75, leased from the New York and Lake Erie Railroad. Seven passenger cars built in 1930 for the Delaware, Lackawanna, and Western Railroad were purchased. The line operates from Perry Street Station in Titusville to Rynd Farm Station north of Oil City where there is a connection with the Western New York and Pennsylvania Railroad. Stations were constructed at Drake Well Park and at Petroleum Centre, which is the main area for the Oil Creek State Park.

One

New York Central Railroad

The Erie and North East Railroad was incorporated April 12, 1842, and construction of the 6-foot-wide track gauge line began on July 26, 1849. This line was completed from Erie to the New York State line on January 19, 1852, where it connected with the 4-foot, 8.5-inch standard track gauge New York and Erie Railroad from Buffalo. Erie's first passenger train station was completed in 1851. Train service from Buffalo to Erie began February 22, 1852. On November 23, 1852, the first train operated from Erie to Ashtabula.

The Dunkirk, Warren, and Pittsburgh Railroad was organized in 1867, and the track was laid south from Dunkirk, New York, reaching Falconer, New York, by June 17, 1871. It became the Dunkirk, Allegheny Valley, and Pittsburgh Railroad on December 31, 1872, and later became the Valley branch of the New York Central Railroad. On February 1, 1968, the New York Central Railroad merged with the Pennsylvania Railroad into the Penn Central Transportation Company, which filed for bankruptcy on June 21, 1970, and operated their last passenger train through Erie on April 30, 1971. Amtrak took over the nation's railroad passenger service on May 1, 1971, discontinuing about 50 percent of the railroad passenger service, including service from Toledo, Ohio, via Erie, to Buffalo, New York, marking the end of railroad passenger service for northwestern Pennsylvania.

On May 11, 1971, Amtrak restored passenger train service from Buffalo via Cleveland to Chicago, but the train did not stop in Erie. However, this service was discontinued on January 5, 1972, because of poor patronage and lack of financial support. Passenger service was restored to Erie with a special train run for the news media stopping in Erie at 7:55 p.m. on October 28, 1975. Regular service to Erie resumed on October 31, 1975. The Consolidated Rail Corporation (Conrail), created by the U.S. government to salvage the Penn Central Transportation Company and several other bankrupt railroads, began operation on April 1, 1976. On June 6, 1998, most of Conrail was split between Norfolk Southern Railway and CSX Transportation. The former New York Central Railroad main line through Erie is now operated by CSX Transportation.

N.Y.C. STATION, NORTH EAST, PA.

This is a postcard view of the passenger station in the borough of North East around 1917. The Lake Shore and Michigan Southern Railway opened this station on October 12, 1899. From 1914 to 1960, the station was used by the New York Central Railroad. Since 1970, the station has been preserved by the Lake Shore Railway Historical Society, Inc., with an adjacent public museum. (Lake Shore Railway Historical Society, Inc.)

2597   Lake Shore Depot, Franklin, Pa.

FRANKLIN

A postcard view of the Lake Shore and Michigan Southern Railway passenger station in the city of Franklin shows that it is virtually the same design as the station in North East. The May 28, 1916, New York Central Railroad timetable showed two trips each way Monday through Saturday and one trip each way on Sunday between Franklin and Sutton. There was direct service from Oil City via Franklin and Ashtabula, Ohio, to Chicago.

Lake Shore Station, Franklin, Pa.

Passengers are waiting as the Lake Shore and Michigan Southern Railway train pulls into the Franklin station around 1910. The Jamestown and Franklin Railroad was completed during 1874. With the completion of the line from Ashtabula, Ohio, to Jamestown, Pennsylvania, in 1871, by the Lake Shore and Michigan Southern Railway, there was now a direct connection from the oil fields of Pennsylvania to the oil refineries in Cleveland.

Lake Shore Tunnel, Oil City, Pa.

At the north portal entrance of the Lake Shore and Michigan Southern Railway tunnel, a passenger train is heading for Oil City in this 1910 postcard scene. This tunnel was also used by the Erie Railroad to reach Oil City. Oil City had passenger service connections to Chicago by both railroads.

13

Union Station in Erie is the scene for former president Theodore Roosevelt's special train on August 25, 1910, where he addressed more than 5,000 people, declaring, "I want all the people living along the Great Lakes to help in securing a purification on your water supply. If you don't you will regret it in years to come. You can't afford to put sewage in your drinking water."

Former president Theodore Roosevelt (with his hand raised) is addressing the crowd at Peach and Turnpike Streets in Erie on August 25, 1910, following his arrival in Erie at 9:35 a.m. from Buffalo. The *Erie Dispatch* newspaper of August 26, 1910, noted, "The greatest demonstration that has ever been accorded any visitor to Erie this year was given ex President Theodore Roosevelt at the Union Passenger Station yesterday morning."

An eastbound passenger train is at the Lake Shore and Michigan Southern Railway (New York Central Railroad as of 1916) station at North Girard in this postcard postmarked 1919. To the right of the station, behind the trees, a Cleveland and Erie Railway trolley car is in view. This later became Lake City, and in 2010, the station has survived as a restaurant. (Gerald N. D'Aurora collection.)

D. A. V. and P. R. R. Depot. Warren. Pa.

Passengers are waiting for the train at the Dunkirk and Allegheny Valley and Pittsburgh Railroad station in Warren. This later became the Valley branch of the New York Central Railroad. The June 1916 *Official Guide of the Railways* showed two passenger trains in each direction from Dunkirk, New York, via Warren, to Titusville. (Gerald N. D'Aurora collection.)

NEW YORK CENTRAL SYSTEM
The Water Level Route—You Can Sleep

Table 2—BUFFALO TO CLEVELAND, TOLEDO, ELKHART AND CHICAGO.

July 15, 1936.

(A large, dense westbound passenger timetable listing stations from Buffalo (R.T.) and Bay View through Erie, North Girard, Ashtabula, Cleveland, Sandusky, Toledo, Elkhart, Mishawaka, South Bend, Gary, and on to Chicago (La Salle St.), with numerous train columns numbered 67, 641, 25, 79, 11, X19, 7, 75, 19, 21, 23, 85, 251, 151, 81, 609, 629, 627, 43, 83, 9, 89, 5, 37, 15, including named trains: The Commodore Vanderbilt, Twentieth Century Limited, Southwestern Limited, Cleveland Limited, The Iroquois, Cleveland-Detroit Express, Empire Express, The Mercury, Lake Shore Limited, The Prairie State, The Forest City, The Mohawk, Ohio State Limited, Missourian, with mileages and scheduled times.)

For Parlor, Sleeping and Dining Car Service, see pages 148-152.

* Daily; † daily, except Sunday; ‡ daily, except Monday; § Sunday only; *d* stops daily, except Sunday; *f* stops on signal to discharge or receive passengers; *i* stops only to discharge passengers; FF stops, except Sunday, on signal to receive passengers for Cleveland and beyond; A stops to discharge passengers from Toledo and beyond; FF stops, except Sunday, on signal to receive passengers for Cleveland and beyond; H leaves from Erie R.R. station; J through cars from Pittsburgh leave from Erie R.R. station at 8 45 p.m.; JJ stops until September 20th, inclusive, to receive or discharge passengers for or from Youngstown and P. & L. E. stations; MM stops daily, except Sunday and holidays, at 8 57 p.m.; X stops only to discharge passengers from New York; Z stops Saturday only. + Coupon stations; δ Telegraph stations.

The July 15, 1936, westbound timetable of the New York Central Railroad, from Buffalo via Cleveland to Chicago, showed 12 passenger trains stopping at Erie. The smaller communities of North Girard and North East also had passenger train service along this main line through Erie County, Pennsylvania. A number of westbound passenger trains, including the *Iroquois*, *Southwestern Limited*, and *Twentieth Century Limited*, did not stop at Erie.

16

On April 26, 1936, the Valley branch of the New York Central Railroad had one daily passenger train in each direction from Dunkirk, New York, via Irvineton, to Titusville. The Youngstown branch had three daily trains in each direction from Buffalo, via Erie, Pennsylvania, and Ashtabula, Ohio, to Pittsburgh. The Oil City branch had one daily train in each direction from Cleveland, Ohio, via Osgood, Pennsylvania, to Oil City.

NEW YORK CENTRAL SYSTEM
The Water Level Route — You Can Sleep

NEW YORK CENTRAL SYSTEM

Table 47—ERIE DIVISION.—Valley Branch.

Table 48—FRANKLIN DIVISION.—Youngstown Branch.

Table 49—CLEVELAND DIVISION. Norwalk Branch.

Table 50—FRANKLIN DIVISION. Oil City Branch.

Table 52—Sharon Branch. — From Hubbard to West Middlesex (13 miles). Operated for freight service only.

The Hudson-type New York Central Railroad locomotive No. 5426 with a 4-6-4 wheel arrangement is westbound, powering the Empire State Express at Union Station in Erie on December 7, 1941. Featuring a bullet nose, this was one of 50 class J3a locomotives in the number series 5405 to 5454 built by American Locomotive Company during 1937 and 1938 for high-speed service. (Gerald N. D'Aurora collection.)

This coal tipple, a structure used for loading coal into the tender of a locomotive, is in Lawrence Park Township east of Lawrence Parkway on the New York Central Railroad around 1941. The coal tipple stores the coal above the railroad tracks and by gravity goes into the tender behind the locomotive. (Lawrence Park Historical Society collection.)

On the east side of Erie, in Lawrence Park Township, the New York Central Railroad had this roundhouse east of Lawrence Parkway. The roundhouse (where inspections, maintenance, and repairs were made to steam locomotives) was a circular structure surrounding a turntable, which is a horizontal rotating platform equipped with a railroad track for turning railroad locomotives and rolling stock. (Lawrence Park Historical Society collection.)

18

An eastbound New York Central Railroad freight train is crossing over Lawrence Parkway and Four Mile Creek in Lawrence Park Township, east of the city of Erie, around 1941. New York Central Railroad steam locomotives were designed for speed for the New York to Chicago main line known as the "Water Level Route" from New York City to Chicago, because it had no significant grades. (Gerald N. D'Aurora collection.)

On September 9, 1962, New York Central Railroad 1,500-horsepower type F3A diesel locomotive No. 1628 (built by the Electro-Motive Division of General Motors Corporation at La Grange, Illinois) is westbound at Lawrence Park, a suburban township east of Erie. This was once a four-track main line. (Photograph by Kenneth C. Springirth.)

East of Water Street in Lawrence Park Township finds 1,500-horsepower type F7A diesel locomotive No. 1783 built by the Electro-Motive Division of General Motors Corporation heading up four diesel units on a New York Central freight train on September 9, 1962. (Photograph by Kenneth C. Springirth.)

Passenger train No. 35, the westbound *Iroquois*, is pulling into Union Station in Erie on February 14, 1965, powered by the Electro-Motive Division of General Motors Corporation diesel locomotives 2,250-horsepower type E8A No. 4085 and 2,000-horsepower type E7A No. 4010. This New York Central Railroad passenger train made the New York to Chicago run in 19 hours and 55 minutes. (Photograph by Kenneth C. Springirth.)

NEW YORK CENTRAL SYSTEM
The Water Level Route—You Can Sleep

NEW YORK CENTRAL SYSTEM

Condensed Time-Table—Table I—CHICAGO-NEW YORK AND BOSTON.

Mls.	STATIONS	New York Special	Fifth Avenue-Cleveland Limited	Ohio State Limited	The Wolverine	New England States	The Pacemaker	Twentieth Century Limited	The Mohawk	The Chicagoan
		354-6 Ex.Sat.	◆6 Daily	16 Daily	8 Daily	28 Daily	2 Daily	◆26 Daily	358-40 Daily	90 Daily
		A M	A.M.			P M	P M	P M	P M	P M
0	(La Salle Street Station.) Lve.Chicago (C.S.T.)	9 30	11 00	.....	.....	2 00	4 00	4 00	4 30	10 20
6.6	Lve.Englewood		h11 15			A214	A414	A414	h444	n919
21.6	Lve.Gary (N.Y.C.Station.)	h1005	11 33			A435	5 30	5 30	5 02	10 55
85.5	Lve.South Bend (C.S.T.)		12 35						5 53	12 05
100.5	Lve.Elkhart (E.S.T.)		2 15				7 00	7 00	3 25	1 50
243.6	Lve.Toledo		4 25 P M				9 00	9 00	9 15	4 00
340.2	Lve.Cleveland (Union Term.)		7 05	9 50			11 05	11 05		7 15
347.1	Lve.East Cleveland									
437.6	Lve.Erie		9 02				12 50	12 50		9 10
545.4	Arr.Buffalo (Cent.Term.)	10 30	10 43	12 45	12 50	2 20	2 20		8 10	11 00
545.3	Lve.Buffalo (Cent.Term.)	11 18	11 18	12 57	1 00	2 45	4 49		8 45	11 26
591.3	Lve.Rochester	12 21	12 21	2 12	2 12		5 52		9 34	12 27
691.2	Arr.Syracuse	1 55	1 35	j3 16	3 35	5 04	7 16		11 18	1 54
710.3	Arr.Rome						7 55		11 57	
724.1	Arr.Utica	2 52	2 52				8 10		12 12	2 44
801.7	Arr.Schenectady			◆5 11	5 29	6 18	9 40		1 41	4 09
818.5	Arr.Albany (E.S.T.)	4 40	4 40	5 37	5 55	7 25	10 10	j9 15	2 10	4 35
							28		16 30	◆404

Mls.	STATIONS	▲6	▲6	16	8		2	26	△40	90
818.5	Lve.Albany (E.S.T.)						7 35			4 50
868.3	Arr.Pittsfield						8 36			5 52
920.5	Arr.Springfield						9 48			7 01
974.6	Arr.Worcester						11 02			8 15
1017.6	Arr.Huntington Avenue						12 03			9 16
1018.9	Arr.Boston (South Sta.) (E.S.T.)						12 15			9 35
							P M			P M

Mls.	STATIONS	▲6	▲6	16	8		2	26	△40	90
818.5	Lve.Albany (E.S.T.)	5 00	5 00	5 47	6 05		10 25		2 25	5 00
887.9	Arr.Poughkeepsie	6 08	6 08	6 57	7 13		11 35		3 43	6 15
928.0	Arr.Harmon	f6 57	f6 57	f7 47	f8 02		f1222	i8 34	f5 38	f7 05
946.2	Arr.Yonkers	*7 23	*7 23				d1250		*5 38	*7 31
960.7	Arr.New York (E.S.T.)	7 55	7 55	8 45	9 00		1 20	9 30	5 50	8 05
	(Grand Central Terminal.)	A M	*M	A M	A M		P M	A.M.	Y M	P M

STATIONS	Empire State Express	North Shore Limited	Ohio State Limited	New England States	Twentieth Century Limited	The Wolverine	Cleveland Limited	The Wolverine	Cleveland Limited	Iri Iroquois	The Chicagoan
	◆51 Daily	39 Daily	15 Daily	27 Daily	◆25 Daily	17 Ex. Sat. Sun.	◆57 Fri. Sat. Sun.	19 Sat. only	◆55 Sun. only	35 Daily	◆59 Daily
	A M	Noon	P M			P M	P M	P M	P M	P M	P M
Lve.New York (E.S.T.) Grand Central Terminal	8 45	12 00	3 00	.....		6 00	6 15	7 00	7 45	7 50	11 15
Lve.Yonkers	h912	h1227	n326				*6 41	j7 27	n811	8 16	
Lve.Harmon	h935	12 51	n350			A646	A705	A751	A835	A841	h1206
Lve.Poughkeepsie		1 45	n440				f757	8 50	9 27	9 35	12 15
Arr.Albany (E.S.T.)	11 30	3 18	5 52			9 15	10 05	10 40	10 50	1 40	2 01
		◆405									
		A M	P M								
Lve.Boston (South Station) (E.S.T.)	.....	10 10	3 15								
Lve.Trinity Place	.....	10 15	3 21								
Lve.Worcester	.....	11 15	4 24								
Lve.Springfield	.....	12 25	5 35								
Lve.Pittsfield	.....	1 38	6 45								
Arr.Albany (E.S.T.)	.....	3 10	7 55								

STATIONS	51	39	15	27	25	17	57	19	55	35	59
Lve.Albany (E.S.T.)	11 37	3 33	5 59	8 05	A842	9 22	10 35	10 50	11 05	2 42	2 29
Lve.Schenectady	12 04	4 04	6 27	8 32		9 51	11 17	11 29	11 35		
Lve.Utica	1 15	5 29	7 47	9 44		11 05	12 40	12 50	12 50	4 50	
Lve.Rome			6 19	8 04	10 02		11 24		1 07	1 42	
Lve.Syracuse	2 00	6 28	8 42	10 40	h1053	12 03	1 38	1 51	5 58	4 38	
Lve.Rochester	3 20	8 08	10 08	12 02		1 28		3 24	7 36	6 16	
Arr.Buffalo (Central Terminal.)	4 30	8 08	11 18	1 07		2 39	4 17	4 35	8 55	7 31	
Lve.Buffalo (Central Terminal.)	5 00	9 53	11 42	1 34		3 04	4 44	4 59	9 27	7 57	
Arr.Erie	6 45		1 03				6 05		11 04	9 25	
Arr.East Cleveland									1 05		
Arr.Cleveland (Union Terminal.)	8 50		2 45				8 00		8 00	1 23	11 12
Arr.Toledo						*5 56		8 00		3 52	1 28
Arr.Elkhart (E.S.T.)					*8 13	*7 55				6 07	3 37
Arr.South Bend (C.S.T.)					*7 17	*7 19				5 35	3 00
Arr.Gary (N.Y.C.Station.)	*6 47				*8 26	*8 12		*122		6 45	
Arr.Englewood					*9 00	*9 00		*1 50			
Arr.Chicago (C.S.T.) (La Salle Street Station.)	7 30		9 15		9 00	12 20		2 05		7 25	4 30
	A M		A M		A M	P M		P M		P M	P M

h stops regularly but only to receive passengers; i stops regularly but only to discharge passengers; f stops on signal to receive or discharge passengers for or from Albany and beyond; n stops on signal to receive passengers; z stops Sunday only. • Stops on signal only.
◆ This train does not carry checked baggage. □ Stops on signal to receive or discharge passengers for or from Toledo and beyond. * Stops on signal to receive passengers for Detroit and beyond. ▣ Stops on signal to receive or discharge passengers for or from Buffalo and beyond. ♥ Stops on signal to receive passengers for points beyond Albany. ▲ Carries checked baggage Albany to New York Sundays only. △ Carries checked baggage Albany to New York only. ▣ Will handle checked baggage Chicago to Buffalo. C.S.T.—Central Standard time. E.S.T.—Eastern Standard time.

For Sleeping Car, Sleepercoach, Coach and Dining Car Service, see pages 102-105.

The December 1962 *Official Guide of the Railways* for the New York Central Railroad shows eastbound passenger trains for Buffalo, New York, and beyond stopping in Erie at 12:50 a.m., 9:10 a.m., and 9:02 p.m., and westbound trains for Cleveland, Ohio, and beyond stopping in Erie at 1:03 a.m., 6:05 a.m., 9:25 a.m., 11:04 a.m., and 6:45 p.m. Not all of the trains were shown on this condensed schedule. The fastest passenger train on the New York Central Railroad was the *Twentieth Century Limited*, which made the 960.7-mile trip from New York to Chicago in 16 hours and did not stop in Erie.

A westbound New York Central Railroad freight train, headed by American Locomotive Company type FA-2 diesel locomotive No. 1096, is passing through the snow-covered countryside at the Bort Road overpass east of the borough of North East, Pennsylvania, near the New York State line on March 2, 1963. In the distance is the bridge for Interstate Highway 90. (Photograph by Kenneth C. Springirth.)

Still in the New York Central Railroad paint scheme, the Penn Central Transportation Company's 2,500-horsepower, four-axle diesel locomotive type GP35 No. 2371, built by the Electro-Motive Division of the General Motors Corporation, is leading a freight train through Lawrence Park Township on May 4, 1968. (Photograph by Kenneth C. Springirth.)

On May 4, 1968, diesel locomotives No. 5243 type RS-3 and No. 3362 type FB-2, built by American Locomotive Company, and diesel locomotive No. 1420 type F3A, built by the Electro-Motive Division of General Motors Corporation, are handling a westbound Penn Central Transportation Company (formerly New York Central Railroad) freight train in Lawrence Park Township. (Photograph by Kenneth C. Springirth.)

Gondola cars are being pulled by three Penn Central Transportation Company (formerly New York Central Railroad) diesel units headed by the Electro-Motive Division of General Motors Corporation No. 1715 type F7A at Lawrence Park Township on May 4, 1968. With centralized traffic control (which started in 1956), this four-track main line was reduced to two tracks that were signaled for operation in both directions on both tracks. (Photograph by Kenneth C. Springirth.)

Harborcreek Township, near Moorheadville Road, is the scene for Penn Central Transportation Company's 2,500-horsepower type U25B diesel locomotive No. 2500, built by General Electric Company and powering a freight train on May 4, 1968. In 2010, this locomotive is on display at the Lake Shore Railway Museum in North East, Pennsylvania. (Photograph by Kenneth C. Springirth.)

Near Moorheadville Road in Harborcreek Township is the scene for a Penn Central Transportation Company freight train with type F7A locomotive No. 1688 built by the Electro-Motive Division of General Motors Corporation and still wearing New York Central Railroad colors on May 8, 1968. (Photograph by Kenneth C. Springirth.)

On May 3, 1969, a Penn Central Transportation Company passenger train is passing a freight train at Lawrence Park Township east of the city of Erie on May 3, 1969, headed by type E8A diesel locomotive No. 4065 built by the Electro-Motive Division of General Motors Corporation. (Photograph by Kenneth C. Springirth.)

At the 87 mile marker from Buffalo, Penn Central Transportation Company (formerly New York Central Railroad) diesel unit No. 1694 Electro-Motive Division of General Motors Corporation type F7A is passing through Union Station at Erie on May 3, 1969. (Photograph by Kenneth C. Springirth.)

The train for Milton Shapp, the Democratic candidate for Pennsylvania governor, is at Union Station in Erie on September 21, 1970, powered by Penn Central Transportation Company type E8A diesel locomotive No. 4286 built by the Electro-Motive Division of General Motors Corporation. The train left Harrisburg and made a number of stops before arriving in Erie. (Photograph by Kenneth C. Springirth.)

The patriotically decorated observation car for Milton Shapp's campaign train for Pennsylvania governor is at Union Station in Erie on September 21, 1970. The September 21, 1970, *Erie Daily Times* newspaper reported the train made a three-day tour of western Pennsylvania to emphasize the need for rail transportation. (Photograph by Kenneth C. Springirth.)

On March 21, 1971, a westbound Penn Central Transportation Company freight train is approaching Walbridge Road. The lead diesel unit No. 7795 was a four-axle, 2,000-horsepower type GP38 locomotive built by the Electro-Motive Division of General Motors Corporation. (Photograph by Kenneth C. Springirth.)

Union Station in Erie is the scene for this Penn Central Transportation Company passenger train on April 10, 1971, powered by type E7A locomotive No. 4211 built originally for the Pennsylvania Railroad by the Electro-Motive Division of General Motors Corporation. (Photograph by Kenneth C. Springirth.)

General Electric type U23B diesel locomotive No. 2728 built for Penn Central Transportation Company and the prototype commuter car for the New Haven line of the New York Metropolitan Transportation Authority are on display at the railroad siding serving the Times Publishing Company near Twelfth and Sassafras Street in Erie on September 15, 1972. (Photograph by Kenneth C. Springirth.)

Penn Central Transportation Company diesel unit No. 3267 type GP40 is passing an eastbound freight train in North East on May 13, 1975. This was a four-axle locomotive with a 16-cylinder engine, which generated 3,000 horsepower and was built by the Electro-Motive Division of General Motors Corporation. (Photograph by Kenneth C. Springirth.)

The *Real People Express* makes a 15-minute stop at Union Station in Erie at 9:00 a.m. on May 23, 1983, as noted by this view of the observation car. "Thousands of fans greet cast of Real People in Erie" was the headline in the *Erie Daily Times* newspaper for May 23, 1983. (Photograph by Kenneth C. Springirth.)

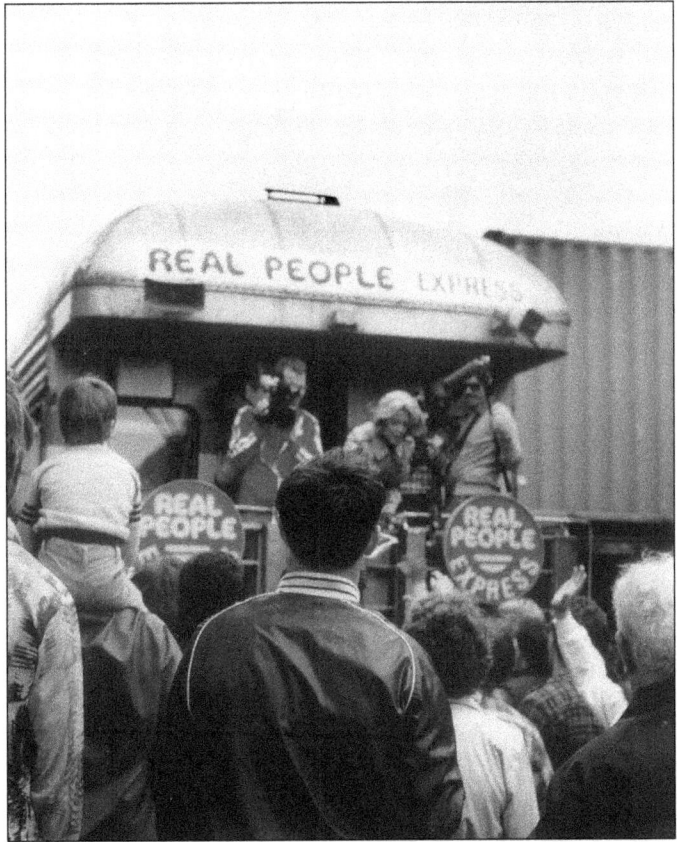

Amtrak's 3,200-horsepower, four-axle type F40PH locomotive No. 353 (built in 1980 by the Electro-Motive Division of General Motors Corporation) is powering the *Real People Express* as it makes a stop in Erie on May 23, 1983, during a 13-state tour from Chicago to Washington, D.C. (Photograph by Kenneth C. Springirth.)

The Ringling Brothers and Barnum and Bailey Circus train is at the Franklin Avenue bridge in Erie for the May 23 and May 24, 1989, show and unloaded at Front and Holland Streets. The May 18, 1989, *Erie Daily Times* noted the animals that will walk about a mile to the Tullio Convention Center "will be six camels, four llamas, four zebras, fifteen horses, and nineteen elephants." (Photograph by Donald Kaverman.)

The westbound National Railroad Passenger Corporation (Amtrak) passenger train is pulling out of Union Station in Erie on January 16, 1999, powered by type P42DC "Genesis" locomotive No. 16 built by General Electric Company. This type of locomotive had a top speed of 110 miles per hour. (Photograph by Donald Kaverman.)

On December 5, 2009, retired railroader J. W. Cray (sitting) and Raymond E. Grabowski, president of the Lake Shore Railway Historical Society, Inc. (standing), are co-owners of this model MT14L speeder, built in 1983 by Fairmount Rail Cars and being used at Christmas at the Station. This was an annual event at the museum's former Lake Shore and Michigan Southern Railway passenger station in North East. (Photograph by Kenneth C. Springirth.)

Christmas at the Lake Shore Railway Museum station in North East on December 6, 2009, finds a General Electric, 25-ton diesel electric locomotive No. 188 (acquired from Ellwood National Forge in 1988) pulling Pennsylvania Railroad flatcar model F36, built in 1941 by the Pennsylvania Railroad, plus Pittsburg and Shawmut Railroad caboose No. 164, built in 1916 by Russell Snow Plow Company. (Photograph by Kenneth C. Springirth.)

An eastbound CSX Transportation freight train powered by two locomotives each having six axles built by General Electric Company is passing through North East, Pennsylvania, on January 17, 2010. Locomotive No. 7602 type Dash 8-40C, rated 4,000 horsepower, was followed by 4,400-horsepower locomotive No. 5447 type ES44DC. (Photograph by Kenneth C. Springirth.)

CSX Transportation diesel unit No. 7896 type Dash 8-41CW, rated 4,135 horsepower, followed by No. 5290 type ES44DC, rated 4,400 horsepower, are heading a freight train ready to cross Walbridge Road in Harborcreek Township on January 26, 2010. General Electric Company built both locomotives. (Photograph by Kenneth C. Springirth.)

Two

PENNSYLVANIA RAILROAD

On April 3, 1837, the Sunbury and Erie Railroad was incorporated. The Sunbury and Erie Railroad opened from Milton to Williamsport on December 15, 1854, and reached Sunbury on January 7, 1856. Service to Lock Haven began July 1, 1859. The first excursion train operated from Erie to Warren on December 15, 1859. On March 7, 1861, by act of the Pennsylvania State Legislature, the Sunbury and Erie Railroad became the Philadelphia and Erie Railroad. On January 1, 1862, the Philadelphia and Erie Railroad was leased to the Pennsylvania Railroad for 999 years. The first passenger train from Philadelphia arrived in Erie with 300 passengers on board on October 5, 1864, at 6:00 p.m. In 1854, construction started in Pittsburgh on the Pittsburgh, Kittanning, and Warren Railroad, which opened for service from Pittsburgh to Kittanning on January 23, 1856, and was completed to Oil City in 1868. The railroad went into receivership in 1884 and reorganized as the Allegheny Valley Railway, which was leased to the Pennsylvania Railroad in 1900. Chartered in 1856, the Erie and Pittsburgh Railroad by 1864 was completed from Erie to New Castle. On March 1, 1870, it was leased to the Pennsylvania Railroad for 999 years. Automobiles began to siphon off passenger traffic in 1920. After 1930, air travel began to attract passengers. The interstate highway system began in 1956 and contributed to the growth of the trucking industry, with a decline in shipping freight by rail. The Penn Central Transportation Company abandoned part of the Erie to Pittsburgh line from Thornton Junction to Sharon on January 1, 1972. On August 13, 1981, the Northeast Rail Services Act of 1981 was enacted, which required that any application to abandon a line filed by Consolidated Rail Corporation before December 1, 1981, would be granted by the Interstate Commerce Commission within 90 days after the date the application was filed unless an offer of financial assistance was made within that 90-day period. Permission to abandon portions of the Erie to Emporium line was granted to Consolidated Rail Corporation, as noted in the *Federal Register* for Tuesday, August 24, 1982, (17.3 miles of track between Johnsonburg and St. Mary effective March 12, 1982) and the *Federal Register* for Tuesday September 14, 1982 (22.5 miles of track from Corry to near Irvine effective June 11, 1982). Consolidated Rail Corporation filed applications to abandon 137 railroad lines in Pennsylvania totaling 725 miles.

In this postcard postmarked December 10, 1907, the Pennsylvania Railroad (formerly Sunbury and Erie Railroad and later Philadelphia and Erie Railroad) passenger train is at the borough of Waterford. The May 28, 1916, schedule showed three northbound trains for Erie stopping at Waterford and three daily southbound trains from Erie stopping at Waterford.

Waterford station (erected in 1860) is the first stop south of Erie on the Philadelphia to Erie line of the Pennsylvania Railroad as shown in this postcard dated December 22, 1909. Railroads provided communities with a link to the outside world, and most people travelled by train. The horse-drawn stagecoach was in place to take travelers to nearby destinations.

A northbound Pennsylvania Railroad train for Erie is preparing to stop at the Union City station in this postcard dated September 17, 1909. The building has survived but is no longer a train station. Only the single track that is closest to the station platform has survived with freight service now provided by the Buffalo and Pittsburgh Railroad.

The Pennsylvania Railroad station in the borough of Union City is shown in this postcard postmarked December 6, 1910. Four daily passenger trains in each direction stopped at this station according to the May 28, 1916, schedule. The railroad made it possible for local products to be shipped to distant markets. Although the freight cars and industrial sidings have disappeared, the station building has survived for other purposes in 2010.

The Pennsylvania Railroad bridge is under construction over the Erie Railroad west of the city of Corry around 1900. The Oil Creek Railroad built the line from Corry via Spartansburg, Centerville, and Hydetown to Titusville. This became the Pennsylvania Railroad, which rebuilt the line going west to Concord, crossing the Erie Railroad on this high bridge and then proceeding south to Spartansburg where it met the original route. (Gerald N. D'Aurora collection.)

DEPOT, CORRY, PA.

Corry is a busy railroad center as shown in this postcard postmarked April 10, 1907. The curved tracks on the left showed Erie Railroad passenger trains. In the center were passenger cars of the Pennsylvania Railroad. In 1916, the Erie Railroad had eight passenger trains stopping at Corry. The Pennsylvania Railroad had six passenger trains (Buffalo to Pittsburgh line) and eight passenger trains (Erie to Philadelphia line) stopping at Corry.

A small number of people are visible on the platform of the Pittsfield station of the Philadelphia and Erie Railroad waiting for the train. Even in a small community, the train station served as a gateway to the outside world and was considered an important public place. On May 1, 1907, the Philadelphia and Erie Railroad was acquired by the Pennsylvania Railroad.

An eastbound Pennsylvania Railroad passenger train is ready to leave the Pittsfield train station in this postcard view. The April 26, 1936, timetable showed two trains in each direction stopping at Pittsfield. This railroad contributed to the growth of population and industry in the counties of Erie, Warren, McKean, Elk, Cameron, Clinton, Lycoming, and Northumberland. (Gerald N. D'Aurora collection.)

Two Pennsylvania Railroad passenger trains have arrived at Irvineton in this postcard postmarked 1913. The train on the left was from Oil City. The train on the right was from Erie. Railroad passenger service peaked in the United States in 1916. (Gerald N. D'Aurora collection.)

The Pennsylvania Railroad station at Irvineton is busy in this postcard dated December 1, 1908. According to the June 1916 *Official Guide of the Railways*, two trains in each direction from Monday to Saturday (one in each direction on Sunday) stopped at Irvineton on the Pennsylvania Railroad line from Olean, New York, to Oil City plus two trains in each direction daily on the Pennsylvania Railroad line from Erie to Philadelphia.

A Pennsylvania Railroad freight train is at the Sheffield station. On the other side of the train platform, the narrow-gauge track of the Tionesta Valley Railway curves off in the distance. Many people have strong personal memories associated with a train station that may have involved a special event in their lives such as farewells for soldiers on their way to military duty. (Sheffield Depot Preservation Society, Inc.)

The Pennsylvania Railroad station in Sheffield is a busy place with passengers waiting for the eastbound passenger train to arrive. A Tionesta Valley Railway engine is on the left side of the station. By the end of 1900, the standard-gauge Sheffield and Tionesta Railroad began operating from Sheffield to Kellettville and reached Tionesta during 1911. Freight was interchanged between all three railroads. (Sheffield Depot Preservation Society, Inc.)

P. R. R. Depot, Youngsville, Pa.

The Pennsylvania Railroad station in the borough of Youngsville is on this postcard postmarked 1914. This was a passenger stop on the Erie to Philadelphia line. The May 28, 1916, schedule showed three trains in each direction stopping at Youngsville. This railroad was one of the earliest large-scale railroad projects in the United States. (Gerald N. D'Aurora collection.)

P. and E. Depot, Sheffield, Pa., Showing Trains of
P. & E. T. V. & S. and T. Railroads.

The eastbound Pennsylvania Railroad passenger train is taking on passengers around 1910 at Sheffield. This station was also used by the standard gauge Sheffield and Tionesta Railway which operated passenger service to the borough of Tionesta. The narrow gauge Tionesta Valley Railway, which operated passenger service to Sheffield Junction, used this station for over 25 years before building its own station west of this station. (Gerald N. D'Aurora collection.)

40

This is a view of the Pennsylvania Railroad station in the city of Warren looking in a southerly direction in this postcard postmarked August 14, 1913. The April 26, 1936, schedule showed three trains in each direction stopping at this station on the former Philadelphia and Erie Railroad. There were two trains in each direction, Monday through Saturday (one in each direction on Sunday), from Oil City via Warren to Olean, New York.

Warren, Pa., Pennsylvania Depot.

At Pennsylvania Avenue looking north, the Pennsylvania Railroad station in Warren is in view in this postcard postmarked September 10, 1908. The number of people at the station as well as the two horse-drawn carriages indicated that a train was expected. The New York Central Railroad also served Warren with its own train station, offering daily service from Dunkirk, New York, via Warren to Titusville.

In this 1910 scene, a Pennsylvania Railroad train is east of downtown Kane passing under the original Baltimore and Ohio Railroad Bridge behind the present-day Kane Area High School. There were two tracks in this scene, and the railroad was originally the Philadelphia and Erie Railroad. The opening of this railroad contributed to the development of many communities in this part of Pennsylvania. (John Marconi collection.)

A Pennsylvania Railroad passenger train is on the steep railroad embankment east of downtown Kane and west of Hemlock Avenue. Located next to the Allegheny National Forest, the borough of Kane is a center for the lumber industry and has been nicknamed "Black Cherry Capital of the World." (John Marconi collection.)

A westbound Pennsylvania Railroad passenger train is arriving at the Kane station. The May 28, 1916, timetable shows four westbound passenger trains and six eastbound passenger trains stopping at Kane. There was a morning train leaving Kane at 6:55 a.m., arriving in Erie at 10:15 a.m., and an afternoon train leaving Erie at 1:00 p.m. and arriving at Kane at 4:20 p.m. The six-story brick building behind the train station known as the New Thomson House was constructed in 1906 and was recognized as a hotel with superior accommodations.

The Pennsylvania Railroad station at Kane, originally built in 1873, is crowded as the train pulls in around 1920. This was an important point on the Erie to Philadelphia line of the Pennsylvania Railroad, becoming a health resort and manufacturing center. Years later, only a handful of passengers used the train service, which made its last run from Erie to Philadelphia on March 27, 1965.

This is an aerial view of the borough of Kane taken around 1970 with the Penn Central Transportation Company (formerly Pennsylvania Railroad) tracks curving around the downtown area. The Poplar Street bridge crossed the railroad yard. Kane, founded in 1864 by Union army general Thomas Leiper Kane, was a manufacturing center with glassworks, bottle works, and lumber mills, plus manufacturers of brush handles, saws, and cutlery. (Kane Historic Preservation Society collection.)

The Poplar Street bridge at Kane is shown over the Pennsylvania Railroad (formerly Philadelphia and Erie Railroad) tracks in this postcard postmarked 1911. On May 23, 1864, the railroad opened from Sheffield to Kane and on July 6, 1864, from Kane southeast to Wilcox. In 2010, only two tracks remain at this location, and nature has reclaimed much of the railroad yard. (Gerald N. D'Aurora collection.)

A northbound Pennsylvania Railroad passenger train is at the busy borough of Johnsonburg station at noontime in this postcard view around 1910. Johnsonburg also had a separate station for the Buffalo, Rochester, and Pittsburgh Railway, which had daily passenger service on its Pittsburgh via Johnsonburg to Buffalo line. (Gerald N. D'Aurora collection.)

The Pennsylvania Railroad station at Johnsonburg is a convenient location for guests of the nearby Hotel Strassley in this view around 1910. Parked at the station was a stagecoach providing local transit service. According to the June 1916 *Official Guide of the Railways*, two trains in each direction stopped at this station on the line from Philadelphia to Erie. The completion of the Philadelphia and Erie Railroad took place west of Johnsonburg, and on August 12, 1864, the first train reached Warren from the east.

P. & E. R. R. Station, Ridgway, Pa.

This postcard, postmarked 1908, features the Pennsylvania Railroad station built in 1907 in the borough of Ridgway. There were three passenger trains stopping at this station each way in the timetable of April 26, 1936. Ridgway, the county seat of Elk County, was founded by Philadelphia shipping merchant Jacob Ridgway. (Gerald N. D'Aurora collection.)

Penna R.R. Station Emporium, Pa.

An eastbound Pennsylvania Railroad passenger train is at the borough of Emporium with a horse-drawn closed wagon at the station providing transportation for passengers and freight parcels to outlying areas. This was a junction point on the Pennsylvania Railroad line from Harrisburg, with one line going north to Buffalo and the other line heading west to Erie. (Gerald N. D'Aurora collection.)

Corydon station is the scene for the Pennsylvania Railroad train in this postcard postmarked 1916. The May 28, 1916, schedule showed two trains in each direction, Monday through Saturday (one on Sunday in each direction), from Olean, New York, via Salamanca, New York, and Corydon, Pennsylvania, to Oil City. (Gerald N. D'Aurora collection.)

A few passengers are waiting for the train at the Pennsylvania Railroad station at Kinzua in this postcard postmarked 1909. When the Kinzua Dam was completed in 1965, this section went under water with the creation of the Allegheny Reservoir and resulted in the abandonment of the line from Warren, Pennsylvania, to Olean, New York. The small towns of Corydon and Kinzua were eliminated with the building of the Kinzua Dam. (Gerald N. D'Aurora collection.)

The Spartansburg passenger station is in view looking north on the Pennsylvania Railroad in this postcard postmarked 1903. Passenger service operated on this line from Buffalo via Corry and Spartansburg to Oil City and Pittsburgh. The April 26, 1936, timetable showed two trains in each direction stopping at Spartansburg. (Gerald N. D'Aurora collection.)

A Pennsylvania Railroad train is involved in a wreck at Titusville on August 12, 1915. The locomotive ran through the Kerr Hill Mill. Kerr Hill was a small community about 2 miles west of Titusville. All forms of transportation have had accidents. The research resulting from many accidents contributed to achieving future safety improvements.

The arrival of a Pennsylvania Railroad passenger train has attracted a number of people at the Titusville train station. Three daily passenger trains stopped at Titusville on the Buffalo to Oil City line according to the April 26, 1936, timetable. Titusville was named for Jonathan Titus, a surveyor for the Holland Land Company, who built his cabin in what is today downtown Titusville. (Gerald N. D'Aurora collection.)

Pennsylvania R. R. Station, Kittanning, Pa.

A number of passengers are by the train at the Pennsylvania Railroad station at the borough of Kittanning in this postcard dated April 3, 1915. The June 1916 *Official Guide of the Railways* showed that the Pennsylvania Railroad had seven passenger trains in each direction from Monday through Saturday (five on Sunday in each direction) stopping at Kittanning, of which three of these trains in each direction operated daily from Pittsburgh via Kittanning to Buffalo, New York.

Union Station in Oil City is the scene for travelers ready to board the arriving Pennsylvania Railroad passenger train. Oil City, on the Allegheny River, prospered with the discovery of oil near Titusville on August 27, 1959. The Pennsylvania, Erie, and New York Central Railroads provided railroad passenger service to Oil City. (Gerald N. D'Aurora collection.)

A Pennsylvania Railroad passenger train is at the borough of Indiana station in this postcard view, which shows a well maintained green space adjacent to the station. The July 20, 1936, schedule showed two trips in each direction daily except Sunday on the Indiana branch from Pittsburgh via Torrance, Blairsville, Black Lick, Coral, Graceton, and Homer City to Indiana.

9128. Pennsylvania R. R. Depot, Greenville, Pa.

Passengers are waiting for the train at the Pennsylvania Railroad station at Greenville in this postcard dated April 12, 1913. During 1916, five southbound (four on Sunday) and five northbound (four on Sunday) passenger trains stopped at this station, of which three trains in each direction (two on Sunday) operated the full length of the line from Pittsburgh to Erie.

Table 173—PITTSBURGH-ERIE.

475	15	455	333	367	415	1639	Mls.	July 12, 1936. (Eastern time.)	404	144	322	332	474	1638	368	424
PM	PM	PM	PM	AM	AM	AM			AM	AM	PM	PM	PM	PM	PM	AM
§5 40	*645	†410	*500	*9 30	*7 25	*521	0	lve.. + **Pittsburgh** ◊..arr.	7 50	10 15	1 30	5 45	7 35	9 20	11 45	11 00
5 45	6 50	4 14	3 05	9 35	7 30	— —	1.0	+ .....Federal Street ... ◊	d746	— —	d125	d541	d750	s915	— —	d1055
6 04	7 07	4 32	— —	9 50	7 48	— —	12.5	+ ..... Sewickley ......◊	7 28	s9 55	1 10	5 27	7 07	9 00	— —	10 35
6 12	7 14	4 43	— —	9 56	7 55	— —	16.4	+ .....Ambridge.........◊	7 16	— —	—	—	6 58	— —	— —	10 30
6 24	7 27	4 56	3 33	10 08	8 10	— —	25.7	+ ..... **Rochester** ......◊	7 01	9 39	12 55	5 11	6 46	8 44	— —	10 19
6 29	7 32	5 01	— —	—	8 15	— —	28.4	+ .....New Brighton.....◊	6 56	— —	12 50	—	6 40	— —	— —	10 15
6 34	7 37	5 06	3 40	10 15	8 20	— —	30.2	+ .....Beaver Falls......◊	6 53	9 31	12 47	5 06	6 37	— —	— —	10 12
—	—	—	—	—	—	—	34.8	..**Homewood Junction**..	f645	— —	—	—	—	—	— —	— —
f6 45	— —	5 17	— —	—	8 32	—	36.3	.........Koppel ....◊	6 40	— —	x1237	—	n626	— —	— —	x1001
—	—	—	—	—	—	—	39.7	.... Crescentdale	—	—	—	—	—	—	—	—
—	—	—	—	—	—	—	40.6	.........Wampum ....◊	—	—	—	—	—	—	—	—
—	—	5 35	— —	—	—	—	47.5	+ .. Cherry St. (New Castle) ..◊	—	—	—	—	—	—	—	—
— —	8 05	— —	4 09	10 45	— —	625	47.6	.. **New Castle Junction**.	— —	9 03	12 20	4 59	— —	8 10	10 37	— —
7 05	822	5 42	421	1057	9 00	637	49.7	arr..+ **New Castle** ◊..lve.	6 15	8 43	12 01	4 19	6 05	7 45	10 17	9 40
7 05	P M	5 42	P M	A M	9 00	A M	49.7	lve.... **New Castle**...arr.	6 15	*AM	*PM	*PM	6 05	*PM	*PM	9 40
f7 19	— —	— —	— —	— —	— —	—	60.0	....Pulaski ....◊	5 56				— —			fg 19
f7 25	— —	— —	— —	— —	— —	—	64.6	....West Middlesex ....◊	f540				— —			fg 13
— —	— —	— —	— —	— —	— —	—	67.4	.........Wheatland ......◊	— —				—			—
7 31		6 06			9 24		68.5	+ .... Farrell ....◊	5 44				5 33			9 06
7 35		6 10			9 32		69.8	+ .... **Sharon**.......◊	f540				5 29			§9 00
P M		P M			9 40		73.0	+ .....Sharpsville......◊	A M				5 16			A M
					— —		75.6	.... Clarksboro ......◊					— —			
					9 48		78.7	+ .... Transfer ......◊					5 04			
					— —		82.8	.........Shenango ......◊					— —			
					10 01		84.4	+ .....Greenville .....◊					4 55			
					10 11		90.5	+ .... .Jamestown .....◊					4 44			
					10 20		96.2	.........Westford ....◊					4 34			
					10 24		99.6	.........Espyville ....◊					4 26			
					10 33		103.6	+ .... **Linesville**.....◊					4 21			
					f1041		107.7	.... Center Road ....◊					4 13			
					10 47		111.2	........Conneautville...◊					4 08			
					10 51		114.0	.... Springboro .....◊					4 03			
					10 59		120.3	.... Albion ....◊					3 55			
					11 16		130.7	........North Girard ....◊					3 40			
					k1123		137.8	.........Swanville.......◊					y3 30			
					11 35		146.0	.........**Erie** ....◊					*3 20			
					A M			[ARRIVE] [LEAVE]					P M			

★ Regularly assigned through cars Air-conditioned.
* Daily; †daily, except Sunday.
§ Sunday only.
a Stops only on signal or notice to agent to receive passengers.
b Stops only on notice to conductor to discharge passengers.
d Stops only to discharge passengers.
e Stops only on notice to conductor to discharge passengers from New Castle Junction and beyond.
f Stops only on signal or notice to agent or conductor to receive or discharge passengers.
k Saturday only.
n Stops on signal Sunday only.
o Stops only on signal or notice to agent to receive passengers for Ravenna and beyond.
s Stops Sunday only.
t Stops only on notice to conductor to discharge passengers from Ravenna and beyond.
u Stops only on notice to conductor to discharge passengers from Harvard Avenue and beyond.
x Stops on signal or notice to agent to receive passengers for Federal Street, Pittsburgh and points beyond.
y Stops only on signal or notice to agent Sunday only to receive passengers for Federal Street, Pittsburgh and points east.
z Stops only on signal or notice to agent to receive passengers for Niles and beyond.

The July 12, 1936, Pennsylvania Railroad timetable shows one daily train in each direction from Erie to Pittsburgh on the Pennsylvania Railroad. The southern portion of the line from Linesville to Pittsburgh had more service, making it possible to take the train to Pittsburgh to get to work.

PENNSYLVANIA RAILROAD
The Standard Railroad of the World

SLEEPING, PARLOR AND DINING CARS—Tables 151, 155 and 159—Continued.
(Coaches on all trains unless otherwise noted.)

No. 578.
Parlor Car ...★Harrisburg to New York. (In No. 54.)
Parlor Coach..★Harrisburg to Washington.
Dining Car..★Harrisburg to New York. (In No. 54.)

Nos. 580 and 580-78—SOUTHERN EXPRESS.
Sleeping Cars..Erie to Philadelphia—(12 S., D. R.). (To No. 580 at Harrisburg.)
★Erie to Washington—(12 S., D. R.). (To No. 50 at Harrisburg.)
★Oil City to New York—(12 S., D. R.). (From No. 951 at Corry to No. 78 at Harrisburg.)
★Rochester to Washington—(12 S., D. R.). (From No. 8420 at Williamsport.) (To No. 50 at Harrisburg.)
★Canandaigua to Philadelphia—(12 S., D. R.). (From No. 8420 at Williamsport to No. 580 at Harrisburg.) (Philadelphia Sleeping Cars may be occupied until 7 00 a.m.)
Dining Cars..★Harrisburg to New York (In No. 78.)
Cafe Coach..★Harrisburg to Washington.
Erie to Renovo.
Through Coach..Erie to Philadelphia. (In No. 580 from Harrisburg.)

No. 630.
Parlor Coach..Williamsport to Philadelphia.
Cafe Coach....Harrisburg to Washington.

No. 8412-570. (See No. 570.)
No. 8418-568. (See No. 568.)
No. 8420-580. (See No. 580.)
No. 8970-570. (See No. 570.)

Nos. 577 and 577-579—INTERNATIONAL EXPRESS.
Sleeping Cars..★Philadelphia to Buffalo—(12 S., D. R.). (Open 9 00 p.m.) (Via Emporium.)
★Washington to Buffalo—(12 S., D. R.) (Open 10 00 p.m.) (Via Emporium.)
Cafe Coach....Williamsport to Buffalo. (Via Emporium.)
Through Coach..Philadelphia to Buffalo. (Via Emporium.)

No. 577-503. (See No. 503.)
No. 579. (See No. 577.)
No. 581—NORTHERN EXPRESS.
Lounge Car..★New York to Harrisburg—(3 C., D. R.). (En route to Chicago in No. 23.)
Sleeping Cars..★New York to Oil City—(12 S., D. R.). (From No. 23 at Harrisburg.) (To No. 950 at Corry.)
Philadelphia to Erie—(12 S., D. R.). (From No. 575 at Harrisburg.)
★Washington to Erie—(12 S., D. R.).
Dining Car..,★New York to Harrisburg. (In No. 23.)
Washington to Harrisburg
Cafe Coach....Renovo to Erie.
Through Coach..Philadelphia to Erie. (From No. 575 at Harrisburg.)

No. 631—WILLIAMSPORT EXPRESS.
Lounge Car..★New York to Harrisburg. (In No. 79.)
Parlor Coach...Philadelphia to Williamsport (week-days).
Dining Car..★New York to Harrisburg. (In No. 79.)
Cafe Coach...Philadelphia to Harrisburg.
Washington to Harrisburg. (Leaving Washington 1 40 p.m.)

★Regularly assigned equipment Air-Conditioned.

EXPLANATION OF SIGNS.

* Daily.
† Daily, except Sunday
§ Sunday only.
⟋ Stops only on signal or notice to agent or conductor to receive or discharge passengers.
▪ Will not run July 4th or September 7th.
● Saturday and Sunday only.
+ Coupon stations.
ᶑ Telegraph stations.

Table 160—BUFFALO AND OIL CITY. Central Region

912	902	950	Mls.	April 26, 1936.	913	903	951
P M	A M			(Central Terminal.)	A M	P M	
*1045	*8 50	....	0	lve...+ Buffalo ᶑ ..arr.	7 25	5 45	....
—	—	....	7.5	+....Blasdell ...ᶑ	—	f5 13	....
—	9 43	....	32.7	+... Silver Creek .. ᶑ	—	4 42	....
11 56	9 58	....	43.3	+.... Dunkirk .... ᶑ	5 53	4 26	....
—	10 09	....	50.8	+.... Brocton .... ᶑ	—	4 15	....
—	f10 30	....	64.2	Mayville Junction..	—	f5 49	....
12 32	10 38	....	65.1	..... Mayville..... ᶑ	5 13	5 44	....
				(Chautauqua Lake)			
—	10 53	....	74.6	+....Sherman.... ᶑ	4 55	5 28	....
—	f11 04	....	81.5	+....Panama .... ᶑ	—	f5 17	....
—	11 13	....	85.8	+....Clymer .... ᶑ	—	5 10	....
1 16	11 25	A M	94.3	arr. + Corry ᶑ ..lve.	4 17	2 57	P M
1 31	11 36	*8 15	94.3	lve.... Corry ....arr.	4 03	2 40	6 48
—	11 51	8 33	103.5	+...Spartansburg... ᶑ	—	2 24	6 28
—	—	f8 39	107.7	.....Glynden..... ᶑ	—	—	f6 23
—	12 01	8 45	111.0	+....Centerville... ᶑ	—	2 15	6 16
—	—	8 49	113.2	....Tryonville.... ᶑ	—	—	f6 09
—	—	8 57	118.4	....Hydetown.... ᶑ	—	—	f6 02
2 15	12 17	9 05	121.9	+....Titusville.....	3 22	1 58	5 55
—	—	f9 17	127.3	....Miller Farm ...	—	—	f5 42
—	—	f9 27	131.0	..Petroleum Centre. ᶑ	—	—	f5 32
—	—	9 35	....	+....Rouseville.... ᶑ	—	—	5 22
3 00	12 55	9 45	138.8	arr...+ Oil City ᶑ ..lve.	*2 45	*1 22	*5 15
3 15	1 05	A M	138.8	lve.... Oil City.....arr.	2 25	1 10	P M
6 55	6 10	....	270.6	arr.+ Pittsburgh .lve.	*10 40	*9 20	....
A M	P M	....		(Eastern time.)	P M	A M	....

Table 161—BUFFALO DIVISION.—Olean and Oil City.

No. 9556	9552	Mls.	April 26, 1936.	No. 9551	9555
....			(Eastern time.)	....	▪P M
....	†7 00	0	lve.. + Olean ᶑ .arr.	....	4 00
....	7 30	3.0	+....Allegany... ᶑ	....	3 35
....	f7 43	9.2	....Vandalia.... ᶑ	....	f3 22
....	....	21.0	lve.+ Bradford ᶑ.arr.	....	....
....	f7 52	11.6	..Riverside Junc...	....	f3 15
....	8 15	19.3	+.. Salamanca .. ᶑ	....	3 00
....	8 35	25.2	+...Red House... ᶑ	....	2 50
....	8 45	31.1	+..Quaker Bridge. ᶑ	....	2 30
....	f8 55	33.2	....Wolf Run .. ᶑ	....	f2 20
....	9 12	36.4	....Onoville	....	2 10
....	9 25	39.7	....Corydon.... ᶑ	....	2 00
....	f9 35	43.1	....Gawango....	....	f1 50
....	f9 45	45.6	...Sugar Run... ᶑ	....	f1 40
....	f10 15	47.7	+....Kinzua.... ᶑ	....	1 30
....	f10 25	51.0	....Big Bend....	....	f1 10
....	f10 45	53.9	....Hemlock.... ᶑ	....	f1 00
....	f11 20	59.2	....Struthers... ᶑ	11 55 A M	f12 25
*3 05 P M	11 40	60.4	+.... Warren .... ᶑ	11 45 ▪	12 10
3 15 ▪	A M	66.2	ar.+ Irvineton ᶑ lv.	11 45 ▪	P M
3 15 ▪	....	66.2	lve.. Irvineton ..arr.	11 45 ▪	....
f3 27 ▪	....	72.6	....Althom.... ᶑ	f11 33 ▪	.....
3 41 ▪	....	80.9	+...Tidioute ... ᶑ	11 19 ▪	.....
3 55 ▪	....	89.5	+..West Hickory . ᶑ	11 03 ▪	.....
f4 03 ▪	....	94.2	....Jamison	f10 54 ▪	.....
4 08 ▪	....	95.8	+....Tionesta... ᶑ	10 49 ▪	.....
f4 14 ▪	....	98.6	....Hunter....	f10 43 ▪	.....
f4 22 ▪	....	102.9	....President....	10 35 ▪	.....
f4 26 ▪	....	104.1	....Eagle Rock...	f10 31 ▪	.....
4 55 P M	....	116.3	+.... Oil City ... ᶑ	*10 05 A M	.....
	....		ARRIVE ⟍ LEAVE		
3 15 A M	....		lve... Oil City ..arr.	2 25 A M	.....
3 33 ▪	....		arr.+ Franklin..lve.	2 08 A M	.....
6 43 ▪	....		arr.+ East Liberty.lve.	10 52 P M	.....
6 55 A M	....		ar.+ Pittsburgh..lv.	*10 40 P M	.....
			(Eastern time.)		

Table 163—BUFFALO DIVISION.—Rochester and Olean.

	9559	9552	Mls.	April 26, 1936.	9557	9555
.....	▪P M	A M	....	(Penna. Station.)	▪P M	P M
.....	†6 50	*8 00	0	lve..+ Rochester ᶑ.arr.	3 20	7 55
.....	f6 15	....		....Scottsville.. ᶑ	f1 55	f6 55

THROUGH CAR SERVICE. (Table 160.)
(Coaches on all trains.)

No. 912—Sleeping Cars ★Buffalo to Pittsburgh—12-Section, Drawing-room (open 9 00 p.m.). Through Coach Buffalo to Pittsburgh.

No. 913—Sleeping Cars ★Pittsburgh to Buffalo—12-Section, Drawing-room (open 9 00 p.m.; may be occupied until 8 00 a.m.). Through Coach Pittsburgh to Buffalo.

No. 950—Sleeping Car ★New York to Oil City—12-Section, Drawing-room (running on Central Division No. 581. Arrive Corry 7 55 a.m.).

No. 951—Sleeping Car ★Oil City to New York—12-Section, Drawing-room (on Central Division No. 580. Leave Corry 7 17 p.m.).

The Pennsylvania Railroad schedule for April 26, 1936, shows two daily through passenger trains in each direction from Buffalo, New York, via Corry, Titusville, and Oil City to Pittsburgh. There was also one daily local train in each direction making all the stops from Corry to Oil City. The Buffalo division from Warren via Tionesta to Oil City had one daily trip in each direction while the section from Warren to Olean, New York, had one daily except Sunday trip. There was a sleeping car from New York to Oil City and from Oil City to New York. The Buffalo to Pittsburgh line also had sleeping car service.

PENNSYLVANIA RAILROAD
Largest Fleet of Air-Conditioned Trains in the World

Eastern and Central Regions

For Through Car Service, see pages 299-300.

151—PHILADELPHIA, WASHINGTON, PITTSBURGH, HARRISBURG, WILLIAMSPORT AND ERIE.

April 26, 1936.

Eastern time.

(Extensive multi-column passenger train timetable with columns for trains 575/581, 575-581, 23-581, 79-631, 78-50/8971, 631, 15-571-8971, No. 553, 61-503, 61-503, 577-605, 577-579, 577, Mls., train numbers 580-78, 580, 574, 576, 630, 578, 8970-570, 568-18-6, 506-6, 506-580; stations listed include New York, Penna. Sta., Hudson Ter., North Phila., Phila. (Broad St.), Phila. (30th St.), Paoli, Lancaster, Harrisburg, Washington, York, Pittsburgh, Sunbury, Northumberland, Montandon, Milton, Watsontown, Dewart, Montgomery, Muncy, Market Street, Williamsport, Newberry, Nisbet, Jersey Shore, Pine, McElhattan, Lock Haven, Farrandsville, Ferney, Glen Union, Hyner, North Bend, Renovo, Shintown, Westport, Keating, Sinnemahoning, Driftwood, Sterling Run, Emporium, Olean, Buffalo, St. Marys, Daguscahonda, Ridgway, Johnsonburg, Wilcox, Dahoga, Sergeant, Kane, Ludlow, Sheffield, Clarendon, Warren, Irvineton, Youngsville, Pittsfield, Garland, Spring Creek, Corry, Elgin, Union City, Waterford, Erie.)

Table 152—SUNBURY AND MOUNT CARMEL.

April 26, 1936.

(Timetable with columns Bus, Bus, 8710, Bus, Bus, Mls.; stations LEAVE Sunbury (P. R. R. Sta.), Hamilton, Keefer, Stonington, Snydertown, Reed, Paxinos, Shamokin (P. R. R. Sta.), Mt. Carmel (P. R. R. Sta.), Mt. Carmel (3rd & Oak Sts.) ARRIVE; and columns Bus, 8711, Bus, Bus, Bus.)

Three daily passenger trains in each direction are shown on the April 26, 1936, Pennsylvania Railroad train schedule from Philadelphia to Erie. There was additional passenger train service from Philadelphia to Williamsport. It was still possible for residents in Kane, Sheffield, Warren, Youngsville, Corry, and Union City to take the morning train to Erie and return by train in the evening.

Two Pennsylvania Railroad 9700 series shark nose diesel locomotives built by Baldwin Lima Hamilton Company are heading southbound at XC Tower, crossing the main line of the New York Central Railroad in Erie. This was a busy railroad serving the harbor along Lake Erie, as Erie was an important manufacturing center. (Gerald N. D'Aurora collection.)

The Pennsylvania Railroad timetable for October 31, 1948, shows that Oil City had an afternoon train No. 980 to Buffalo, which made a connection in Corry with train No. 580 for Baltimore, Washington, D.C., Philadelphia, and New York. In the morning, there was train No. 981 from Buffalo, which made a connection in Corry with train No. 581 from New York, Philadelphia, Baltimore, and Washington, D.C., to reach Oil City.

Pennsylvania Railroad type RS3 diesel locomotive No. 8468 is at Corry in this November 6, 1962, scene. This was a 1,600-horsepower road switcher built by American Locomotive Company in 1952. (Photograph by Kenneth C. Springirth.)

On February 14, 1965, the Pennsylvania Railroad passenger train No. 581, the *Northern Express*, has arrived at Union Station in Erie. When Erie's Union Station was dedicated on December 3, 1927, there was a daylong celebration. The New York Central Railroad spent $1.5 million for the station and an additional $4.5 million to elevate the railroad tracks and depress adjacent streets. (Photograph by Kenneth C. Springirth.)

Pennsylvania Railroad passenger train No. 580, the *Southern Express*, is crossing Norcross Road in Millcreek Township, bound for Philadelphia on March 17, 1963. The Pennsylvania Railroad used a standard Tuscan red (a brick-colored shade of red) for passenger cars and most of their passenger hauling diesel locomotives. Lettering after World War II was done in buff yellow (a light shade of yellow). (Photograph by Kenneth C. Springirth.)

The *Northern Express* passenger train is about to pass under Shannon Road in Harborcreek Township for its morning run to Erie on March 20, 1965. During World War II, the Pennsylvania Railroad carried huge volumes of freight and passenger traffic. With passenger traffic declining, this train had only one more week left before discontinuance. (Photograph by Kenneth C. Springirth.)

Pennsylvania Railroad type E8A diesel locomotive No. 5703 is crossing under Interstate 90 on its final morning trip to Erie on Saturday, March 27, 1965. Passenger service from Erie to Philadelphia ended on Saturday, March 27, 1965, when train No. 580 left Erie at 5:45 p.m. "A Fond Farewell to a Proud Train" was the headline in the *Erie Times-News* newspaper for March 28, 1965. (Photograph by Kenneth C. Springirth.)

An ex-Pennsylvania Railroad snowplow is at the Penn Central Transportation Company yards in Erie on August 17, 1969. Manufactured by Russell Snowplow Company of Ridgway, Pennsylvania, the snowplow had large wings set into the body on each side behind the front "V" blade to handle the heavy winter snow along the Great Lakes, a cupola (windowed projection on the roof) for the operator, and a headlight for night operations. (Photograph by Kenneth C. Springirth.)

At Wayne Street yards in Erie, a Penn Central Transportation Company diesel locomotive No. 1865 is waiting for the next assignment on June 16, 1973. Built by the Electro-Motive Division of General Motors Corporation, this type F7A locomotive was rated at 1,500 horsepower and was used in both freight and passenger service. (Photograph by Kenneth C. Springirth.)

On the turntable at the Penn Central Transportation Company yards at Wayne Street in Erie on May 13, 1975, are type GP7 four-axle, 1,500-horsepower diesel locomotive No. 5600 and 1,200-horsepower type SW7 diesel switcher No. 9064, both built by the Electro-Motive Division of General Motors Corporation. (Photograph by Kenneth C. Springirth.)

On October 22, 1978, Consolidated Rail Corporation diesels Nos. 7713 and 7716 are at the East yard in Erie. Both units were four-axle, 2,000-horsepower type GP38 diesel locomotives originally built for the Penn Central Transportation Company by the Electro-Motive Division of General Motors Corporation. (Photograph by Kenneth C. Springirth.)

An Erie to Warren freight train is crossing Norcross Road in Millcreek Township on March 28, 1982, powered by Consolidated Rail Corporation diesel locomotive No. 2192. This was a four-axle, 2,250-horsepower type GP30 locomotive originally built for the New York Central Railroad by the Electro-Motive Division of General Motors Corporation. (Photograph by Kenneth C. Springirth.)

A westbound Consolidated Rail Corporation freight train powered by diesel locomotive No. 7554 is crossing the former main line of the Erie Lackawanna Railroad in Corry on October 2, 1982. This four-axle, 1,750-horsepower type GP9 locomotive was originally built for the New York, New Haven, and Hartford Railroad by the Electro-Motive Division of General Motors Corporation. (Photograph by Kenneth C. Springirth.)

On October 2, 1982, Consolidated Rail Corporation diesel No. 7554 with tank car and caboose is at the siding in Corry west of the crossing of the former main line of the Erie Lackawanna Railroad. This was the former Erie to Emporium branch of the Pennsylvania Railroad. (Photograph by Kenneth C. Springirth.)

Allegheny Railroad type GP40 locomotives Nos. 102 and 101 are at the Kane station on a special "Rail Freight Awareness Program" train that operated from Warren to Kane and back to Warren on September 11, 1986. The railroad was a 150-mile subsidiary of Hammermill Paper Company that began operating on September 3, 1985, over the former Pennsylvania Railroad from Erie to Emporium. (Photograph by Kenneth C. Springirth.)

An eastbound Allegheny Railroad freight train is coming through Corry powered by the four-axle, 3,000-horsepower type GP40 locomotives Nos. 302 and 3111 on September 7, 1996. Genesee and Wyoming, Inc., purchased this railroad and renamed it Allegheny and Eastern Railroad. In 2004, it was merged into the Buffalo and Pittsburgh Railroad, which is also owned by Genesee and Wyoming, Inc. (Photograph by Kenneth C. Springirth.)

The former Pennsylvania Railroad station is in Kane in this February 7, 2010, view. The Kane Historic Preservation Society has restored the station. Major projects included repair and replacement of the roof, installation of a central climate controlled system, replacement of both chimneys, window repairs, installation of safety storm windows, maple flooring installation, handicap restroom installation, cleaning and repairing brick work, and exterior and interior painting. (Photograph by Kenneth C. Springirth.)

Pictured on February 21, 2010, the former Pennsylvania Railroad station, built in 1880 and closed in 1965, was restored by the Sheffield Depot Preservation Society, Inc. The work included a massive cleanup of the building, every window pane of glass was replaced (160 panes of glass), lights were installed, the ticket room floor was replaced, the interior was repainted, and certain areas were insulated. (Photograph by Kenneth C. Springirth.)

Three

NICKEL PLATE ROAD

The Buffalo, Cleveland, and Chicago Railway was incorporated in October 1880 and on April 13, 1881, was consolidated into the New York, Chicago, and St. Louis Railroad to build a railroad from Buffalo via Erie to Chicago. From Buffalo to Cleveland, it would parallel the Lake Shore and Michigan Southern Railway. It became known as the Nickel Plate Road from an article in the Norwalk, Ohio, *Chronicle* of March 10, 1881, which reported the arrival of a party of engineers to take a survey for the "great New York and St. Louis double track, nickel plated railroad." In 1882, the railroad recognized F. R. Loomis, owner and editor of the Norwalk *Chronicle*, as originator of the term and issued him a complimentary railroad pass.

In Erie, there were problems in securing a city franchise. The March 7, 1881, *Erie Morning Dispatch* noted that a few property owners on Nineteenth Street opposed the railroad right-of-way on Nineteenth Street, because they would not be compensated for damage to their property. By a 16 to 7 vote, Erie's Common Council approved the railroad's request to use Nineteenth Street for their right-of-way through Erie according to the May 21, 1881, *Erie Morning Dispatch*. The 28-mile section from Conneaut, Ohio, to Erie was constructed during February and March 1882. Train service began on October 23, 1882. In 1959, the railroad's heaviest passenger business was east of Cleveland, because train schedules allowed shoppers from Erie and Ashtabula to spend a full day in Cleveland. The completion of Interstate 90 west to Cleveland meant Erie was a two-hour drive from Cleveland, and railroad passenger ridership declined. The last *New Yorker* passenger train left Chicago on June 2, 1963. The last *Westerner* passenger train left Buffalo on June 3, 1963. Effective October 16, 1964, the Nickel Plate Road merged into the Norfolk and Western Railway. The former Nickel Plate Road's last passenger trains, *City of Chicago* and *City of Cleveland*, were discontinued on September 9, 1965. On December 31, 1990, the Norfolk and Western Railway and Southern Railway became the Norfolk Southern Railway.

NICKEL PLATE ROAD
THE NEW YORK, CHICAGO AND ST. LOUIS RAILROAD COMPANY

Table No. 1.
NEW YORK, BUFFALO, CLEVELAND AND CHICAGO.

No. 9 Note B	No. 5 Note B	No. 7 Note B	Mls.	April 26, 1936.	No. 8	No. 6 Note 0	10-6
				(Eastern time.)			
				LEAVE [ARRIVE			
*1 00 A M	*1000 A M	*6 00 P M		..New York (Lackawanna)..	*8 04 A M	*5 42 A M	*5 42 A M
				(Eastern time.)			
				LEAVE [ARRIVE			
*1245 P M	*7 45 P M	*4 30 A M	0	d/☐+..Buffalo, N. Y...☐	10 05 P M	1 25 P M	1 25 P M
			21.6	....Angola.......	☐-	☐-	- -
f1 28 »	☐-	- -	31.5	+....Silver Creek..☐	- -	9 ″	9 ″
1 42 »	h842 »	a-	41.1	+....Dunkirk......☐	☐859 »	f1219 P M	f1219 P M
- -	☐-	- -	49.6	+....Brocton.....☐	″	″	- -
- -		- -	50.7	....Portland.....☐	-	-	- -
v204 »	☐-	- -	57.6	{..+Westfield☐	b-	f1157 A M	f1157 A M
v214 »	☐-	- -	65.6	(H—Chautauqua, N. Y.) }..Ripley, N.Y..	j-	j-	- -
2 25 »	☐-	- -	73.3	+...North East, Pa...☐	f137 »	f1137 »	- -
2 45 »	9 85 »	6 10 »	87.0	+.....Erie.......☐	807 »	11 18 »	11 18 »
v ▽		- -	98.2	+....Fairview....☐	-	j-	j-
v507 »	☐-	- -	101.5	...X Wallace Junction..☐	b-	A-	- -
- -	☐-	- -	102.2	....Girard.......☐	b-	A-	- -
- -	☐-	- -	105.0	...Thornton Junction..☐	-	A-	- -
- -	☐-	- -	106.8	....East Springfield, Pa...☐	-	j-	- -
3 30 »	10 18 »	6 53 »	115.1	dl+...Conneaut, O...☐	7 55 »	A-	- -
- -		- -	122.5	+.....Kingsville....☐	-	A-	- -
3 50 »	10 37 »	7 13 »	128.2	+....Ashtabula...☐	7 12 »	10 09 »	10 09 »
x557 »		- -	133.5	+....Saybrook.....☐	b-	j-	j-
f4 02 »		- -	137.8	+....Geneva.......☐	-	j-	- -
v406 »		- -	143.2	+....Madison......☐	b-	j-	- -
f4 21 »	fH05 »	f7 44 »	154.9	+....Painesville..☐	b-	f9 32 »	f9 32 »
- -		- -	159.0	....Mentor......☐	-	A-	- -
f4 34 »	☐-	f7 57 »	164.9	+....Willoughby...☐	-	f9 18 »	f9 18 »
- -		- -	169.0	....Wickliffe....☐	-	-	- -
- -		- -	176.6	....Euclid......☐	-	A-	- -
4 52 »	11 54 »	8 15 »	177.1	+.East Cleveland (Superior Ave.).☐	6 17 »	8 59 »	8 59 »
5 15 P M	11 57 P M	8 40 A M	184.1	arr..+ Cleveland ☐..lve.	6 01 P M	8 40 A M	8 40 A M
				(Union Terminal.)			
				(Union Terminal.)			
5 25 P M	12 00 A M	8 30 A M	184.1	lve....Cleveland.....arr.	5 51 P M	8 10 A M	8 25 A M
5 50 »	12 35 »	9 15 »	192.8	+....Rocky River..☐	5 25 »	7 38 »	7 58 »
- -		- -	197.4	....North Dover..☐	-	-	- -
- -		- -	202.5	.....Avon.......☐	-	-	- -
6 15 »	1 00 »	9 40 »	210.8	+.....Lorain.....☐	5 04 »	7 18 »	7 36 »
- -		- -	221.5	+....Vermillion...☐	-	-	- -
- -		- -	229.5	....Berlin Heights..☐	-	-	- -
- -		- -	231.0	....Shinrock.....☐	-	-	- -
- -		- -	236.4	.....Avery......☐	-	-	- -
- -		- -	240.5	+....Kimball.....☐	-	-	- -
7 04 »	1 55 »	10 28 »	248.2	l+....Bellevue...☐	4 20 »	6 30 »	6 51 »
- -	- -	- -	260.4	+.. Green Springs Jn..☐	○-	-	- -
- -		- -	265.3	....Old Fort......☐	○-	-	- -
- -		- -	269.7	....Maple Grove...☐	-	-	- -
7 53 P M	2 38 A M	11 11 »	280.7	+.....Fostoria....☐	5 37 »	5 41 A M	*6 07 A M
f-	f-	- -	286.4	+.....Arcadia.....☐	c-	c-	-
f-	f-	11 29 A M	293.3	..Mortimer (Findlay)..☐	f-	c-	-
f-	f-	- -	300.0	+.....McComb.....☐	3 09 P M	-	-
f-	f-	- -	310.8	arr..Leipsic Junction.lve.	t-	t-	-
				(Eastern time.)			
				(Central time.)			
f-	f-	- -	310.8	lv.+.Leipsic Junction☐..arr.	t-	t-	-
f-	f-	- -	311.7	+.....Leipsic.....☐	-	-	-
f-	f-	- -	318.7	....Millers City...☐	-	-	-
f-	f-	11 14 A M	325.8	+...Continental...☐	f-	-	-
f-	c-	- -	331.6	+.....Oakwood.....☐	f-	-	-
f-		- -	333.9	+.....Melrose.....☐	-	-	-
f-	☆-	- -	342.3	+.......Latty.....☐	c-	-	-
f-	f-	- -	349.8	+....Payne, O.....☐	f-	-	-
f-		- -	354.1	....Edgerton, Ind..☐	-	-	-
f-		- -	365.0	....New Haven.....☐	-	-	-
3 40 A M	12 15 P M	372.6	+....Fort Wayne ☐..lve.	12 49 P M	2 13 A M	
3 52 »	12 18 »	372.6	lve..Fort Wayne....arr.	12 44 P M	2 31 »	
- -			387.1	.....Raber......☐	f-	-	
	4 26 »		390.0	....Peabody......☐	f-	-	
- -			397.3	....South Whitley..☐	f-	-	
- -			403.5	+.....Sidney.....☐	f-	-	
- -		o-	406.5	+...Packertown...☐	f-	-	
- -			411.1	+.....Claypool...☐	f-	-	
- -			416.0	....Burket.......☐	f-	-	
- -			419.8	+....Mentone.....☐	f-	-	
- -			424.4	....Tippecanoe...☐	-	-	
- -			431.0	+......Argos.....☐	t-	-	
f5 18 »	g1 47 »	432.0	+...Hibbard (Culver)..☐	f1129 A M	-	
- -			440.6	+....Burr Oak.....☐	-	-	
5 37 »	2 05 »	451.8	+......Knox......☐	11 15 »	102 A M	
- -			463.2	....Thomaston....☐	-	-	
- -			468.2	...South Wanatah..☐	-	-	
j-		f2 32 »	477.3	+...Valparaiso....☐	f-	-	
j-			488.4	......Hobart......☐	f-	-	
j-	3 06 »	493.2	....South Gary....☐	▽-	-	
6 44 »			503.9	+....Hammond, Ind..☐	10 35 »	11 59 P M	
- -			512.6	....Stony Island, Ill..☐	f-	-	
7 15 »	3 35 »	517.1	+....Englewood...☐	9 53 »	11 33 »	
7 35 A M	3 55 P M	523.8	+.....Chicago....☐	*9 40 A M	*1120 P M	
				ARRIVE] (Cent. time.) [LEAVE			

For time of trains Nos. 9 and 10 between Buffalo and St. Louis, see Table 1a.

Table No. 1a.
ST. LOUIS AND CLEVELAND.

No. 10	Mls.	April 26, 1936.	No. 9
See Note D		LEAVE [ARRIVE	See Note E
*6 10 P M	0	+St. Louis (Union Sta.)..	7 35 A M
6 18 »		...Washington Avenue, Mo...	7 04 »
⊙		+..East St. Louis, Ill...	⊙
6 52 »	21.5	+....Edwardsville.......	6 13 »
- -	46.6	+.....Sorento.......	5 38 »
e8 00 »	74.8	+.....Ramsey........	5 02 »
8 17 »	134.4	arr..+Charleston..lve.	3 35 »
8 17 »	134.4	lve..Charleston....arr.	3 30 »
- -	140.0	+....Fair Grange....	- -
- -	142.1	.....Bushton.......	- -
- -	146.3	......Rardin.......	- -
- -	149.8	+.....Oakland......	- -
- -	150.1	+.....Brocton......	- -
- -	164.9	+.....Metcalf......	- -
- -	175.6	+....Ridge Farm....	- -
- -	181.5	+.....Humrick......	- -
10 31 »	186.9	+....Cayuga, Ind....	2 10 »
- -	190.2	....Silverwood.....	- -
10 55 »	194.9	......Cates........	- -
- -	204.3	+...Veedersburg....	1 50 »
- -	211.7	+.....Mellott......	- -
- -	215.7	+.....Wingate......	- -
- -	221.0	+...New Richmond...	- -
11 25 P M	224.9	+......Linden......	1 21 »
- -	229.7	+....Kirkpatrick...	- -
- -	235.6	+....Clark's Hill...	- -
- -	243.1	......Jefferson....	- -
at212 A M	247.2	arr..+ Frankfort..lve.	at1245 »
12 15 »	247.2	lve....Frankfort...arr.	12 35 A M
- -	253.7	+....Boylestone....	- -
- -	256.6	+....Hillsburg.....	- -
- -	258.8	+....Scircleville..	- -
- -	262.5	+....Kempton......	- -
- -	266.7	+....Goldsmith.....	- -
12 49 »	272.4	+......Tipton......	11 47 P M
- -	277.3	......Hobbs.......	- -
f1 03 »	283.0	+.....Elwood......	f11 24 »
f1 13 »	291.8	+....Alexandria...	f11 12 »
- -	297.3	......Gilman......	- -
1 40 »	308.0	+......Muncie.....	10 35 »
- -	314.5	+....De Soto......	- -
- -	319.6	+......Albany.....	- -
- -	325.0	+....Red Key......	- -
f2 14 »	335.9	+.....Portland....	9 50 »
- -	346.9	+..Fort Recovery, O...	- -
2 43 »	356.1	+....Coldwater....	9 18 »
a57 »	361.8	+......Celina.....	9 08 »
3 10 »	371.6	+....St. Marys.....	8 52 »
- -	380.7	......Buckland....	- -
- -	384.6	........Hume......	- -
- -	391.4	.....South Lima...	- -
3 55 »	392.9	arr.+Lima (Cent. time)..lve.	8 10 »
4 55 »	392.9	lve..Lima (East. time)...arr.	8 10 »
- -	402.0	....Beaver Dam....	- -
ρ-	408.1	+.....Bluffton....	ρ-
- -	412.5	....Mount Cory....	- -
- -	415.2	+......Rawson.....	- -
5 45 »	424.1	+......Findlay....	8 25 »
- -	433.1	+.....Arcadia.....	- -
6 07 »	438.8	+.....Fostoria....	7 53 »
- -	449.8	....Maple Grove...	- -
- -	454.2	....Old Fort......	- -
- -	459.1	+..Green Springs Junc...	- -
6 51 »	471.3	+.....Bellevue....	7 04 »
- -	478.6	+......Kimball....	- -
- -	484.3	.......Avery......	- -
- -	488.4	......Shinrock....	- -
- -	489.9	...Berlin Heights...	- -
- -	498.0	....Vermillion....	- -
7 38 »	503.7	+......Lorain.....	6 15 »
- -	517.0	........Avon......	- -
- -	522.1	....North Dover...	- -
7 56 »	526.7	+..Rocky River (Lakewood)..	5 50 »
8 25 A M	535.4	+..Cleveland (Union Term.)..	*6 25 P M
		ARRIVE] [LEAVE	

No. 6

*8 40 A M		lv. Cleveland (Union Term.) ar.	5 15 P M
11 18 A M		lve.....Erie.....lve.	2 45 »
1 25 P M		arr....Buffalo....lve.	12 45 P M
5 42 A M		..New York (Lackawanna)..	*1 00 A M
		ARRIVE] [LEAVE	

Nos. 10-6 and 9 — 8-Section and Observation Lounge (Radio) (Air-conditioned) Sleeping Cars between St. Louis and Cleveland. 12-Section Drawing-room Sleeping Car (Air-conditioned) Cleveland to New York. Sleeping Car New York to Buffalo. 12-Section Drawing-room. Cleveland and the Virginias. (see table No. 3). Dining Car. Coaches (Ladies' lounge).

For Explanation of Signs, see page 428.

The April 26, 1936, schedule for the New York, Chicago, and St. Louis Railroad Company, known as the Nickel Plate Road, shows three daily westbound and two daily eastbound passenger trains operating through Erie on the Buffalo to Chicago main line. Using the Nickel Plate Road from New York to Chicago required taking the Delaware, Lackawanna, and Western Railroad from New York to Buffalo and transferring to the Nickel Plate Road at Buffalo.

Nickel Plate Road type S-4 switcher No. 74 is in Erie on a local switching assignment on November 6, 1962. American Locomotive Company built this 1,000-horsepower locomotive in May 1953, and it was retired on June 14, 1972. (Photograph by Kenneth C. Springirth.)

The eastbound *City of Cleveland* is in Erie on November 6, 1962, headed by type GP9 diesel locomotive No. 482, built by the Electro-Motive Division of General Motors Corporation. A hard core of riders continued to use the train because of the railroad's convenient service and modern equipment. (Photograph by Kenneth C. Springirth.)

Walbridge Road, in Harborcreek Township east of Erie, is the scene for Nickel Plate Road passenger train *City of Cleveland* heading east to Buffalo, New York, on July 4, 1963. With the discontinuance of the *Westerner* and *New Yorker* in June 1963, there was only one passenger train in each direction on the Buffalo to Chicago line. (Photograph by Kenneth C. Springirth.)

New York, Chicago, and St. Louis Railroad passenger train No. 6, *City of Cleveland*, is at the Erie station on September 6, 1964, eastbound to Buffalo. Type GP9 diesel locomotive No. 477 was built by the Electro-Motive Division of General Motors Corporation in July 1955 and was retired April 22, 1985. Passenger service on this railroad made its last run through Erie on September 9, 1965. (Photograph by Kenneth C. Springirth.)

Norfolk and Western Railway type GP35 diesel locomotive No. 1316, built by the Electro-Motive Division of General Motors Corporation, is handling a westbound freight train at Moorheadville Road crossing in Harborcreek Township on May 8, 1968, close to the parallel Penn Central Transportation Company main line. (Photograph by Kenneth C. Springirth.)

Along the Nineteenth Street trackage between Peach and Sassafras Streets in downtown Erie, Nickel Plate Road steam engine No. 759 has made a passenger stop on September 8, 1968. The Lake Shore Railway Historical Society, Inc., in conjunction with the High Iron Company, sponsored the excursion from Conneaut, Ohio, to Buffalo, New York. Lima Locomotive Works built this class S-2 locomotive in August 1944. (Photograph by Kenneth C. Springirth.)

The bridge near East Avenue in Erie is the scene for Nickel Plate Road steam locomotive No. 759 handling an eastbound excursion train from Conneaut, Ohio, to Buffalo, New York, on September 8, 1968. This Berkshire-type locomotive had a 2-8-4 wheel arrangement with one unpowered leading axle followed by four powered driving axles and two unpowered trailing axles. (Photograph by Kenneth C. Springirth.)

Nickel Plate Road steam locomotive No. 759 is speeding by East Avenue in Erie on an excursion to Buffalo, New York, on September 8, 1968. The locomotive had 69-inch-diameter driver wheels, a total weight of 440,800 pounds, and had a tractive effort of 64,100 pounds, which is the force that a locomotive can apply to its coupler to pull a train. (Photograph by Kenneth C. Springirth.)

On September 8, 1968, Berkshire-type steam locomotive No. 759 is near Brickyard Road in North East Township on the Norfolk and Western Railway excursion to Buffalo, New York. This was one of 15 locomotives numbered 755 to 769 that were built by Lima Locomotive Works during 1944. The locomotive is now at the Steamtown National Historic Site in Scranton, Pennsylvania. (Photograph by Kenneth C. Springirth.)

Steam locomotive No. 759 is in North East, Pennsylvania, powering the excursion train to Buffalo, New York, on September 8, 1968. American Locomotive Company built 15 of these locomotives, numbered 700 to 714, in 1934. The Lima Hamilton Corporation built the last 10, numbered 770 to 779, at a cost per locomotive of $226,315.10, which was 2.5 times the cost of the 700 to 714 series locomotives. (Photograph by Kenneth C. Springirth.)

The Golden Spike Centennial Limited, using former Nickel Plate Road steam locomotive No. 759, with two symbols of a golden spike painted on the front, is on Nineteenth Street near Peach Street in Erie on the Norfolk and Western Railway on May 4, 1969. The train was westbound for Promontory Summit, Utah, to celebrate the 100th anniversary of the completion of the transcontinental railroad. (Photograph by Kenneth C. Springirth.)

On October 3, 1973, the Nickel Plate Road passenger station in Erie, built around 1883 at Nineteenth and Holland Streets, is devoid of any passengers. The October 28, 1962, Nickel Plate Road passenger schedule showed two trains in each direction from Chicago via Erie to Buffalo allowing a one-day trip from Erie to Buffalo or Cleveland. Passenger train service on this line ended on September 9, 1965. (Photograph by Kenneth C. Springirth.)

The American Freedom Train is at Lake Shore Railway Museum station in North East on Penn Central Transportation Company tracks for a refueling stop on May 13, 1975. Using former Reading Railroad steam locomotive No. 2101, the train was westbound for Cleveland, Ohio. From April 1, 1975, to December 31, 1976, over seven million people visited the train on its tour of 48 states. (Photograph by Kenneth C. Springirth.)

Norfolk and Western Railway diesel locomotive No. 8079 (a six-axle, 3,000-horsepower General Electric Company type C30-7 locomotive) and Electro-Motive Division of General Motors Corporation type FP7 Southern Railway 1,500-horsepower diesel No. 6141 are in North East heading a passenger excursion on July 22, 1980, sponsored by the Lake Shore Railway Historical Society, Inc., from Erie via North East to Buffalo with a return trip. (Photograph by Kenneth C. Springirth.)

On August 11, 1984, Norfolk and Western Railway steam locomotive No. 611 is in Erie for an excursion to Buffalo, New York, sponsored by the Lake Shore Railway Historical Society, Inc. This streamlined steam locomotive with a 4-8-4 wheel arrangement was designed and built at the Norfolk and Western Railway shops in Roanoke, Virginia, in May 1950. (Photograph by Kenneth C. Springirth.)

On August 3, 1986, the observation car is at the end of the excursion train of the Lake Shore Railway Historical Society, Inc., on the Nineteenth Street trackage in Erie. Using Norfolk and Western Railway steam locomotive No. 611, the train operated from Erie via Conneaut, Ohio, to Bellevue, Ohio. The railroad operated 1.2 miles in the center of Nineteenth Street from Raspberry to Peach Streets. (Photograph by Kenneth C. Springirth.)

A replica of the "Best Friend of Charleston" is on the Norfolk Southern Railway in North East, Pennsylvania, on September 27, 1986. The original train made its first trip on December 25, 1830, in Charleston, South Carolina, becoming the first steam locomotive in the United States to operate scheduled passenger service. It was destroyed in a boiler explosion but replaced in 1928 by a replica. (Photograph by Kenneth C. Springirth.)

On October 12, 2001, a special Norfolk Southern Railway passenger train, powered by 3,000-horsepower type SD40-2 locomotive No. 3376, is at Nineteenth Street and Greengarden Road in Erie to make a last run over the Nineteenth Street trackage from Greengarden Road to Parade Street. The railroad relocated 5.15 miles of its trackage to the CSX Transportation railroad right-of-way from East Avenue to Pittsburgh Avenue. (Photograph by Donald Kaverman.)

Erie mayor Joyce Savocchio (her back in the picture) and a Norfolk Southern Railway track worker are at Nineteenth and Parade Streets on October 12, 2001, where the first section of track has been removed in the ceremony attended by the public and news media, marking the beginning of the removal of the Nineteenth Street railroad tracks. The last freight train passed over these tracks on September 27, 2001. (Photograph by Donald Kaverman.)

An eastbound Norfolk Southern Railway freight train is ready to cross Walbridge Road in Harborcreek Township on January 26, 2010. General Electric Company built both six-axle, 4,000-horsepower locomotives with No. 9902, a type Dash 9-40CW, and No. 7518, a type ES40DC. (Photograph by Kenneth C. Springirth.)

74

Four

ERIE RAILROAD

The 6-foot-wide track gauge Atlantic and Great Western Railroad reached Corry in June 1861 and Meadville in 1862. It was believed the wide-gauge track would prevent traffic from being lost to other lines. The line from Meadville to Franklin opened in May 1863 and reached Oil City in March 1865. In March 1880, the New York, Pennsylvania, and Ohio Railroad was organized from the bankrupt Atlantic and Great Western Railroad. On March 6, 1883, the New York, Lake Erie, and Western Railroad leased the New York, Pennsylvania, and Ohio Railroad. It was changed to standard gauge in 1884. On June 28, 1887, the first railroad car of fruits ever to reach New York from California arrived in New York via Meadville by this railroad. In 1893, the New York, Lake Erie, and Western Railroad went into bankruptcy reorganization and emerged as the Erie Railroad on November 6, 1895. The line through Corry and Meadville became the Erie Railroad's main line to Chicago. On May 28, 1952, the Erie Railroad dedicated a new passenger station in Corry. A large crowd was in attendance to hear Erie Railroad president Paul W. Johnston declare, "We want Corry to grow and prosper" because the Erie Railroad depends on cities like this and hundreds of others. David A. Hillstrom, president and founder of Corry Jamestown Corporation, was master of ceremonies and praised the Erie Railroad for its progress in the city and predicted the station would be welcomed as an addition to the city's civic improvement, which should be viewed with pride. Other speakers included Corry mayor J. Fred Kinley and Stewart A. Long, president of the Corry Chamber of Commerce. The mayor's wife, Alma Kinley, cut the ribbon.

Under the Consolidated Rail Corporation, portions of the line from Corry, Pennsylvania, to Jamestown, New York, and between Olean and Hornell, New York, were taken out of service with approval given by the Interstate Commerce Commission to abandon the section from Meadville to Corry in August 1994. The Northwest Pennsylvania Railroad Authority purchased 41.6 miles of track from Meadville to Corry on October 31, 1995, and in January 2002 sold it to the Western New York and Pennsylvania Railroad, which in December 2005 leased the Norfolk Southern Railway line from Meadville to Oil City and now operates from Rouseville via Oil City and Meadville to Hornell, New York.

Erie Depot, Union City, Pa.

The Erie Railroad station in Union City shows plenty of freight cars in this postcard view dated September 2, 1909. This was on the New York to Chicago main line of the railroad. The August 1936 *Official Guide of the Railways* showed two westbound trains and three eastbound trains stopping at this station.

Erie Depot, Cochranton, Pa.

Many passengers are at the borough of Cochranton station of the Erie Railroad for the northbound train to Meadville in this postcard dated 1908. The June 1916 *Official Guide of the Railways* showed four trains in each direction, Monday through Saturday (three in each direction on Sunday), from Meadville via Cochranton to Oil City. (Gerald N. D'Aurora collection.)

76

An Erie Railroad passenger train has arrived at the Meadville train station in this postcard dated March 10, 1908. The station was built in 1896 and was torn down during 1972. Meadville had daily passenger service east to New York and west to Chicago and Cleveland. In addition, there was local passenger service from Meadville to Oil City.

Three daily trains in each direction stopped at the Erie Railroad station in the borough of Cambridge Springs according to the June 1916 *Official Guide of the Railways*. The Erie Railroad was the first railroad to ship milk to New York City in 1842, the first railroad to use iron rails rolled in America in 1847, and the first railroad in 1851 to exceed 400 miles in length. (Gerald N. D'Aurora collection.)

Erie R. R. Depot, Franklin, Pa.

The impressive Erie Railroad station in Franklin is the scene for a few people waiting for the train to pull into the station in this postcard dated February 28, 1914. Franklin was on the Oil City to Meadville branch, which had daily passenger service.

Erie Depot and train Five, Greenville, Pa.

Erie Railroad passenger train No. 5 is westbound at Greenville on its trip from New York to Cleveland in this postcard view around 1915. The June 1916 *Official Guide of the Railways* showed five passenger trains in each direction, Monday to Saturday (Sunday had four westbound and three eastbound), stopping at this Greenville station. The passenger station is now a Norfolk Southern Railway maintenance facility. Today the Greenville Railroad Park and Museum at 314 Main Street in Greenville is on the right side of the picture.

Erie R. R. Station and Motor Car,
Bradford, Pa.

Erie Railroad gasoline-powered railcar No. 4002 is at the city of Bradford train station pulling a trailer around 1915. Built by McKeen Motor Car Company, the 70-foot-long, 200-horsepower railcar operated between Bradford, Pennsylvania, and Salamanca, New York, from 1909 to 1922. The steel-bodied center entrance railcar with ship-like porthole windows was designed by William McKeen, superintendent of Motive Power for the Union Pacific Railroad.

8830. Erie R. R. Round House, looking West, Meadville, Pa.

A number of steam locomotives are in view at the Erie Railroad roundhouse looking west in Meadville. With the distance from New York to Chicago at 999 miles, Meadville was almost at the halfway point at 517 miles from New York. This made it a natural location to locate engine facilities and shops. Meadville, located where Cussewago Creek flows into the French Creek, was founded on May 12, 1788, by a group of settlers led by David Mead. (Gerald N. D'Aurora collection.)

2179   Erie R. R. Shops, Meadville, Pa.

A number of steam locomotives are ready for service in this view taken around 1920 at the Meadville shops of the Erie Railroad. During the time period between 1901 and 1926, the Erie Railroad was almost completely rebuilt east of Meadville and operating expenses were reduced 11 percent by running longer and heavier freight trains.

Erie R. R. Station, Meadville, Pa.

A crowd of people are at the Erie Railroad station in Meadville waiting for the next train around 1920. Meadville had direct train service east to New York, west to Cleveland and Chicago, and a branch line to Oil City. The Erie Railroad took pride in providing dependable passenger service.

Well-maintained Mead Park made an inviting entranceway to the Erie Railroad station in Meadville around 1920. Meadville was an important city on the Erie Railroad as evidenced by the large station. The Erie Railroad showed its respect for passengers by providing an attractive passenger station in Meadville.

An eastbound Erie Railroad train is in Corry around 1955, and on the right side of the picture, a Pennsylvania Railroad passenger train is in view. The Corry passenger station, west of the visible freight house, was the last new passenger station built in Erie County, Pennsylvania, and was dedicated on May 28, 1952.

Erie Railroad

STANDARD—Eastern time New York to Lima. Central time west of Lima.

For Through New York-Chicago Schedules, see Table 1.

Table 8. SALAMANCA-CHICAGO.

5	4	7	Miles.	June 14, 1936.	2	8	6	620		
				Eastern time.						
P M	A M	P M			P M		A M			
*7 00	*8 05	*1035	0	lv. {New (+West 23d St.).ar.	7 45	P M	8 05			
7 20	8 10	11 30		York(+Chambers St..ar.	7 54	11 54	7 54			
7 45	8 30	11 45	2	..Jersey City....lv.	7 20	11 40	7 40			
A M	P M	A M		**Eastern time.**	A M	P M	P M			
*6 15	*6 45	*1115	413.6	lve..+Salamanca ō..arr.	9 05	1 11	8 27			
6 35			432.2	+....Randolph....		1250				
7 00	7 55	12 10	447.3	ar.Jamestown(Chaut.L.)iv.	8 25	12 16	8 48			
	P M	A M		lve...Buffalo...arr.	A M	P M				
	*8 05	*8 05		(Lehigh Valley Term.)	1050	7 05				
7 00	7 55	12 10	447.3	lve...Jamestown ō..arr.	8 25	12 16	8 48			
				(Chautauqua Lake)						
7 37	8 11	12 49	474.4	+....Corry....ō	7 46	11 25	8 07			
7 53	8 25	—	485.8	+..Union City....ō	7 28	11 06	7 50			
8 23	*8 45	1 23	501.8	+..Cambridge Springs.ō	7 08	10 41	7 32			
8 32	9 05	1 41	516.0	ar.+Meadville ō...lve.	6 50	10 20	7 13			
9 55	10 20			arr...Franklin...lve.	5 35		5 55			
10 15	10 40			arr...Oil City...lve.	*5 15		*5 30			
8 37	8 08	1 46	516.0	lve...Meadville ō	6 45	10 15	7 09			
9 14	8 47	2 24	542.1	+...Greenville...ō	6 08	9 43	6 31			
9 36	10 16	2 51	558.1	+....Sharon....ō	5 35	9 12	6 06			
			564.4	+....Hubbard....ō	—	—	9 58			
9 58	*1058	3 12	571.8	ar.+Youngstown ō.lv.	5 07	*8 50	6 43	9 45		
1 53	—	6 55		Pittsburgh (P.&L.E.RR.)			*7 15	2 20	6 15	
P M		P M		**ARRIVE**	**LEAVE**		P M	P M	P M	
10 08	*10 45	3 19	571.8	lve..Youngstown...arr.	4 57	*8 45	5 59	9 40		
	—		576.3	+....Girard....ō	—	*9 32				
10 22	*1055	—	580.5	+....Niles....ō	8 20	9 26				
10 34	11 10	3 41	585.7	+...Warren...ō	*1140	8 21	9 17			
11 45			638.1	ar...Cleveland...lv.	*4 00	*8 00				
A M				**ARRIVE**	**LEAVE**	P M	P M			
11 59	4 24	—	609.6	+....Ravenna....ō	—	7 53				
12 13	4 44	—	615.9	+....Kent....ō	4 05	7 42				
—	*463	—	625.9	+....Akron....ō	3 44	7 22				
—	—	—	633.3	+..Barberton....	—	7 04				
—	—	—	640.0	+..Wadsworth....	—	6 52				
1 22	5 13	—	644.6	+....Rittman....	—	6 48				
1 22	5 58	—	676.1	+....Ashland....ō	2 32	6 05				
1 54	6 55	—	693.1	+...Mansfield...ō	2 02	5 38				
2 22	7 10	—	708.5	+....Galion....ō	1 39	5 00				
2 37	7 36	—	729.4	arr..+Marion..ō..lve.	1258	4 39				
2 54	7 51	—	729.4	lve...Marion...arr.	1253	4 34				
—	8 06	—	754.4	+....Kenton....ō	—	4 04				
3 52	9 06	—	781.5	+....Lima....ō	11 56	3 30				
				(Eastern time.)						
				(Central time.)						
—	—	—	794.2	+..Spencerville..ō	10 12	—				
—	—	—	808.7	+...Ohio City...ō	8 48	1 32				
3 52	—	—	825.5	+...Decatur...ō	8 48	1 32				
4 25	8 40	—	836.0	arr.+Huntington ō.lve.	8 10	12 58				
4 30	9 00	—	836.0	lve...Huntington...arr.	8 00	1253				
5 22	—	—	897.8	+...Rochester...ō	8 14	—				
6 33	—	—	961.5	+..Crown Point..ō	7 05	—				
6 55	12 15	—	977.7	+..Hammond..ō	6 40	10 40				
27 17	*1243	991.9		+..Englewood.(63d St.)..	5 15	*1015				
7 35	1 00		998.5	ar.+Chicago (C.T.)ō lv.	*6 00	*1000				
A M	A M			(Dearborn Station.)	P M	P M				

Table 7—SALAMANCA-DUNKIRK.

5—527	Mls.	June 14, 1936.	540
		Eastern time.	
P M	0	lve...New York...arr.	
‖7 00		+....West 23d Street...	
7 20		+..Chambers Street...	
‖7 45	2.0	+...Jersey City...	
‖603	413.6	arr.+Salamanca..lve.	
Mix.		**LEAVE**	Mix.
A M			P M
‖7 00	0	+...Salamanca...	5 15
7 35	8.2	+..Little Valley...	4 55
8 30	15.5	+..Cattaraugus...	4 50
8 45	21.9	+....Persia....	4 00
9 05	24.9	arr...Dayton...lve.	5 50
10 50		arr....Buffalo....lve.	
9 30	24.9	lve...Dayton...arr.	5 40
9 40	27.8	+..Perrysburg..ō	5 50
9 45	30.8	+..West Perrysburg..ō	5 20
9 55	36.8	+..Smith's Mills..ō	5 10
10 10	38.6	+..Forestville..	3 00
10 25	42.9	+..Sheridan..	2 45
10 40	46.8	arr...Dunkirk...lve.	12 30
A M		**ARRIVE**	**LEAVE** P M

Table 9—ELMIRA-CORNING-ROCHESTER.

5—463	7—467	Mls.	June 14, 1936.	468—464	8
			Eastern time.		
P M	P M	0	lve...New York...arr.		
‖700	‖1055		+....West 23d Street....	P M	P M
7 80	‖1130		+..Chambers Street..	1154	1154
7 45	‖1145	2.0	+...Jersey City...	1140	1140
A M	A M		**Eastern time.**	A M	A M
§2 35	§712	0	lve...Elmira...arr.	5 15	5 15
3 00	7 44		+..Corning ō..lve.	4 47	4 47
3 30	8 00	0	lve...Corning...arr.	4 10	4 00
3 37	8 07	2.1	+..Painted Post...ō	3 58	3 50
3 43	8 13	3.2	+...Cooper's...ō	3 56	3 41
3 53	8 23	9.5	+...Campbell...ō	3 41	3 32
4 02	8 32	14.1	+...Savona...ō	3 21	3 00
4 16	8 45	20.4	+....Bath....ō	3 11	2 60
4 23	8 53	24.1	+...Kanona...ō	2 55	2 59
4 30	9 01	27.8	+...Avoca...ō	2 45	2 14
4 35	9 07	30.6	+..Wallace..ō	2 33	2 09
4 45	9 16	35.5	+..Cohocton..ō	2 22	1 58
4 52	9 25	39.8	+...Atlanta...ō	2 08	1 44
5 02	9 35	45.8	+...Wayland...ō	1 58	1 34
5 10	9 43	50.5	+..Springwater..ō	1 48	1 26
5 26	9 52	53.2	+..Websters..ō	1 29	1 26
5 34	9 57	57.2	+..Conesus..ō	1 25	‖1248
5 43	‖1004	60.9	+.South Livonia..ō	1 17	12 42
5 51	10 11	64.5	+...Livonia...ō	1 11	12 36
5 56	10 17	67.2	+..South Lima..ō	1 05	‖1230
—	—	69.0	Conesus Lake Junc...	—	‖1226
6 15	10 32	76.2	arr...Avon ō...lve.	12 46	‖1252
A M	10 40	81.4	+...Avon...arr.	12 41	A M
—	10 50	82.1	+...Golah...	—	
—	10 54	82.7	+..Industry..ō	12 31	
—	‖1059	85.0	+.West Henrietta..ō		
—	11 15	94.8	arr...Rochester...ō	‖1210	
	A M		arr. (Erie Depot) lve.	P M	

Table 12—SALAMANCA-BRADFORD.

The Allegany Motor Coach Company, Inc.						557	Mls	June 14, 1936.	560			The Allegany Motor Coach Company, Inc.			
	P M	P M	P M	P M	P M	A M		**Eastern time.**	P M	A M	A M	Noon	P M	P M	P M
	*8 15	*1035	*7 10	*5 40	*4 30	*2 20	*9 35	*8 20	*6 20	0	lve.+Salamanca.arr.	8 10	8 55	9 02 9 55 1200 3 02 5 12 5 20
							6 30	5.4	+..Carrollton..		8 55			
							6 43	12.9	+..Limestone ..		8 45			
							16 51	15.9	+.East Bradford..		18 36			
	11 67	11 10	7 45	6 25	5 16	3 00	10 15	9 00	6 55	17.2	+..Bradford..ō	*6 35	*8 15	8 17
	P M	P M	P M	P M	P M	A M	A M	A M	A M		**ARRIVE**	**LEAVE**	P M	P M

Table 14—ROCHESTER-MOUNT MORRIS.

424	420	440	416	428	468	408	404	Mls.	June 14, 1936.	425	401	403	467	409	416	419
⊙P M	⊙#	⊙P M	⊙P M	⊙#	P M	A M	⊙#		LVE. (E.T.) ARR.	⊙#	⊙#	A M	A M	⊙#	P M	⊙P M
*1020	†615	*515	415	4 25	*120			0	+...Rochester...ō	5 35	745	8 45	11 15	1 00	5 00	7 50
10 39	9 27	5 25	4 25	1 35	—	9 30	730	4.7	+...Mortimer..	5 25	7 30	8 27	—	1245	4 45	7 56
10 57	6 53	5 33	4 34	1 45	—	9 37	740	8.9	+.West Henrietta..ō	6 18	7 22	8 18	1059	1259	4 54	7 27
10 45	6 46	5 40	4 42	150	1231	9 43	746	12.1	+...Industry...ō	6 12	7 15	8 12	10 54	1231	4 27	7 19
10 46	6 51	5 45	4 47		1 55	9 48	751	14.4	+....Golah....	6 07	7 10	8 09	—	1222	4 22	7 15
10 57	7 04	5 55	5 00	204	1201	9 56	800	18.6	arr..Avon ō..lve.	1600	7 02	8 00	10 54	1216	4 15	7 04
10 57	7 04	5 55	5 00	204		9 56	A M		lve...Avon...arr.	A M	7 02	8 00	A M	1216	4 15	7 04
11 15	7 21	6 11	5 21	223		1012		27.5	+...Geneseo...ō	6 42	7 43		11 58	5 58	6 47	
11 25	7 55	6 25	5 55	235		1025		33.0	+.Mount Morris..	1630	*730		†1145	*340	*635	
P M	P M	P M	P M	P M		A M			**ARRIVE**	A M	A M		A M	P M	P M	

* Daily; †daily, except Sunday; ‡daily, except Saturday; ‖daily,except Monday; §Sunday only.
a Stops on signal to receive passengers for New York.
f Stops on signal to receive and discharge passengers.
h Stops on signal to discharge passengers from Chicago and to receive passengers for Jamestown and east.
s Saturday only.
u Stops on signal to receive passengers for Mansfield and west.
t Stops on signal to leave passengers from Chicago and to receive for Binghamton and east.

x Stops to leave passengers from east of Avon.
y Stops on signal to receive passengers for east of Hammond.
z Stops to discharge passengers from east of Hammond.
‡ Will not run holidays.
⊡ Via Dodaro Bus Co.
• No baggage carried.
⊙ Mixed train between Corning and Avon.

* Stops on signal to leave from Jamestown and east and to take for Youngstown and west.
+ Coupon stations.
ō Telegraph stations.

The June 14, 1936, Erie Railroad passenger schedule shows three daily trains in each direction stopping at Corry, Cambridge Springs, Meadville, Greenville, and Sharon, of which two trains in each direction went from New York to Chicago and one train in each direction went from New York to Cleveland. There were two daily trains in each direction from Meadville via Franklin to Oil City. Two westbound trains and three eastbound trains served Union City. The passenger train *Erie Limited* made the New York to Chicago run westbound in 24 hours and 30 minutes and eastbound in 24 hours and 45 minutes.

On November 6, 1962, the Erie-Lackawanna Railroad passenger train *Pacific Express* is in Corry headed by a 2,250-horsepower type E8A diesel locomotive No. 819, built in 1951 originally for the Delaware, Lackawanna, and Western Railroad by the Electro-Motive Division of General Motors Corporation. (Photograph by Kenneth C. Springirth.)

A Railway Express/U.S. mail car and a passenger car are at the end of the Erie-Lackawanna Railroad train *Pacific Express* in Corry on November 6, 1962. Although time was running out for passenger service, the Erie-Lackawanna Railroad was noted for its fine service. A minor renaming occurred in 1963 when the hyphen was dropped and it became Erie Lackawanna Railroad. (Photograph by Kenneth C. Springirth.)

NEW YORK NEWARK THE POCONOS SCRANTON	BINGHAMTON ELMIRA CORNING BUFFALO JAMESTOWN	YOUNGSTOWN CLEVELAND AKRON CHICAGO
WESTBOUND —READ DOWN	TABLE 1	EASTBOUND —READ UP

The Owl 15 N.B. Daily Ex. Sat.	17 N.B. Sat. Nite Only	The Lake Cities 5 Daily	Miles From Hoboken	EASTERN STANDARD TIME	New York Mail 10 N.B. Daily Ex. Sun.	The Lake Cities 6 Daily
PM	PM	PM		NEW YORK, N. Y.	AM	AM
				Via PATH (Port Authority Trans-Hudson)		
11.43	11.13	7.03	.....	Lv. 33rd St. & 6th Ave. .... Ar.	4.06	9.06
11.46	11.11	7.06	.....	" Hudson Term. Bldg., Cortlandt St. .... "	.....	9.06
Ex. Sun.	.....	.....	.....	Lv. Barclay St. Via Ferry .... Ar.	.....	A
12.15	11.45	7.30	0.0	Lv. HOBOKEN, N. J. .... Ar.	3.35	8.45
.....	Sun. Only	7.45	7.8	Lv. Newark, N. J. .... Ar.	3.21	Δ 8.32
.....		7.53	10.6	" Brick Church .... "	.....	Δ 8.23
.....	.....	8.07	20.1	" Summit .... "	.....	Δ 8.09
.....	.....	8.35	40.5	" Dover .... "	2.38	Δ 7.42
.....	.....	a 9.05	67.2	" Blairstown .... Lv.	.....	a 7.10
2.25	1.47	a 9.33	83.9	" East Stroudsburg, Pa. .... "	1.48	a 6.51
.....	.....	a 9.51	97.0	" Cresco .... "	.....	a 6.29
.....	.....	a F10.05	105.0	" Pocono Summit .... "	.....	.....
3.35	3.00	10.45	135.5	Ar. Scranton .... Lv.	12.20	5.39
4.00	3.30	11.00		Lv. Scranton .... Ar.	12.00	5.32
5.10	4.40	12.01	194.1	Ar. Binghamton, N. Y .... Lv.	10.55	4.30
5.40	.....	12.15	194.1	Lv. Binghamton, N. Y. .... Ar.	10.25	4.10
5.54	.....	.....	202.7	" Endicott (Vestal) .... Lv.	10.12	.....
6.13	.....	.....	216.1	" Owego .... "	9.55	.....
6.40	.....	a P12.55	235.8	" Waverly (Sayre, Pa.) .... "	9.34	a Q 3.28
7.00	.....	1.15	252.9	Ar. Elmira .... Lv.	9.10	3.10
7.25	.....	1.30		Lv. Elmira .... Ar.	8.55	3.02
7.58	.....	1.55	271.0	Lv. Corning .... Lv.	8.35	2.44
8.10	.....	.....	281.5	" Addison .... "	.....	.....
8.45	.....	2.40	311.5	Ar. Hornell .... Lv.	7.35	2.02
9.05	.....	↓	311.5	Lv. Hornell .... Ar.	7.20	↑
10.10	.....		355.6	" Warsaw .... Lv.	6.25	
11.15	.....		401.8	Ar. Buffalo (515 Babcock Street) .... Lv.	5.15	
.....	.....	2.50	311.5	Lv. Hornell .... Ar.	.....	1.50
.....	.....	3.27	337.7	" Wellsville .... Lv.	.....	1.17
.....	.....	4.17	374.9	" Olean .... "	.....	12.33
.....	.....	4.40	393.0	Ar. Salamanca .... Lv.	.....	12.10
.....	.....	4.50	393.0	Lv. Salamanca .... Ar.	.....	12.01
.....	.....	a Z 5.09	410.4	" Randolph .... Lv.	.....	.....
.....	.....	5.35	426.8	" Jamestown (Chautauqua Lake) .... "	.....	11.25
.....	.....	6.10	453.5	" Corry, Pa. .... "	.....	10.50
.....	.....	7.05	495.2	Lv. Meadville .... Lv.	.....	10.05
.....	.....	7.40	521.4	" Greenville .... "	.....	9.29
.....	.....	8.01	536.3	" Sharon .... "	.....	9.06
.....	.....	8.23	549.9	Ar. Youngstown, Ohio .... Lv.	.....	8.43
.....	.....	8.40	549.9	Lv. Youngstown, Ohio .... Ar.	.....	8.27
.....	.....	9.01	563.8	Lv. Warren .... Lv.	.....	8.05
.....	.....	K 12.30 ▲	617.1	Ar. Cleveland .... Lv. Union Terminal, Public Square	.....	T 5.20 ▲
.....	.....	9.45	594.2	Lv. Kent .... Lv.	.....	7.30
.....	.....	10.05	604.9	" Akron .... "	.....	7.10
.....	.....	10.57	654.7	" Ashland .... "	.....	6.05
.....	.....	11.25	671.3	" Mansfield .... "	.....	5.48
.....	.....	11.43	686.8	" Galion .... "	.....	5.22
.....	.....	12.05	707.7	Ar. Marion .... Lv.	.....	5.00
.....	.....	12.25	707.7	Lv. Marion .... Ar.	.....	4.40
.....	.....	a 1.20	759.6	" Lima .... Lv.	.....	a 3.50
.....	.....	a 2.45	834.2	Lv. Huntington, Ind. .... Lv.	.....	a 2.28
				CENTRAL STANDARD TIME		
.....	.....	a 2.25	875.9	Lv. Rochester .... Lv.	.....	a 12.43
.....	.....	a 3.40	955.8	" Hammond .... "	.....	a 11.30
.....	.....	4.15	977.0	Ar. CHICAGO, ILL. (Dearborn Station) .. Lv.	.....	10.50
AM	AM	PM			PM	AM

Except Monday Morning

CLEVELAND-WARREN-YOUNGSTOWN

READ DOWN — TABLE 2 — READ UP

28 Daily Ex.Sat., Sun. & Hol.	Miles from Cleveland	EASTERN STANDARD TIME	29 Daily Ex.Sat., Sun. & Hol.
PM		Cleveland, Ohio (See note below)	AM
5.20	0.0	Lv. Union Terminal Public Square .... Ar.	7.40
a 5.29	2.9	" E. 55th St. & McBride Ave. .... Lv.	a 7.32
a 5.40	8.3	" Lee Rd., Shaker Hts. Station .... "	a 7.21
a 5.45	10.3	" North Randall .... "	a 7.16
a 5.52	15.5	" Solon .... "	a 7.10
a 5.59	20.0	" Geauga Lake .... "	a 7.02
a 6.06	23.3	" Aurora .... "	a 6.56
a 6.17	29.7	" Mantua .... "	a 6.45
a 6.24	33.9	" Jeddoe .... "	a 6.38
a 6.30	36.4	" Garrettsville-Hiram .... "	a 6.31
a 6.51	52.3	" Warren .... "	a 6.12
a 6.59	57.4	" Niles .... "	a 6.02
7.10	66.2	Ar. Youngstown .... Lv.	5.50
PM		NOTE: Hand baggage only may be checked to or from Cleveland.	AM

PUBLIC TRANSPORTATION CONNECTIONS BETWEEN HOBOKEN, N. J. TERMINAL AND NEW YORK CITY

PATH (Port Authority Trans-Hudson)—Tube Trains operate between our Hoboken, N. J. Terminal and midtown and downtown New York City. Frequent daily service to and from Christopher St., 9th St., 14th St., 23rd St., and 33rd St.; also, downtown to Hudson Terminal, Cortlandt Street. Trains do not stop at Christopher or 23rd Sts. Sat., Sun. & Hol. Train connections shown in this timetable. Fare 30¢.

PUBLIC SERVICE BUS NO. 63—Buses operate between our Hoboken, N. J. Terminal and the Port Authority Bus Terminal, 8th Avenue at 40th Street, New York City. Frequent service. Fare 40¢.

REDUCED FARES AVAILABLE FOR GROUP TRAVEL

Clubs, churches, organizations and convention groups will find it to their advantage to submit their Travel Plans to the nearest EL RR passenger representative, or write

A. G. OLDENQUIST, Gen'l Psgr. Traffic Mgr.
Erie Lackawanna R. R., Hoboken, N. J.

PASSENGER SALES REPRESENTATIVES

New York, N. Y. 10007 (212) BArclay 7-2500
Hoboken, N. J. 07030 (Terminal Bldg.)
(201) OLdfield 9-2000 or MArket 2-8374
D. CAMPBELL, Div. Pass. Sales Mgr.

Youngstown, O. 44503 (Terminal Bldg.)
Telephone (216) 747-0792
G. T. LAWRENCE, Div. Pass. Sales Mgr.

Chiacgo, Ill. 60604 (327 So. LaSalle St.) (312) HArrison 7-4160
N. A. MITTS, Gen'l. Pass. Agt.

G. W. KROM, Manager Mail, Baggage & Express, Hoboken, N. J.
R. H. TAYLOR, Passenger Traffic Manager, Hoboken, N. J.
A. G. OLDENQUIST, Gen. Pass. Traffic Mgr., Hoboken, N. J.

The Erie Lackawanna Railroad timetable, effective October 29, 1967, shows one daily passenger train, *The Lake Cities*, in each direction from New York via Corry, Meadville, Greenville, and Sharon to Chicago. With the discontinuance of the passenger train *Phoebe Snow* on November 27, 1966, only the passenger train *The Lake Cities* was left for the New York to Chicago service, and it made its last run January 6, 1970. There was a Monday to Friday commuter train service from Youngstown to Cleveland, Ohio, which made its last run on January 14, 1977.

Now under Consolidated Rail Corporation, four-axle, 1,500-horsepower type GP7 locomotive No. 1273 (built by the Electro-Motive Division of General Motors Corporation), in its former Erie Lackawanna Railroad colors, is operating a freight train on the former Erie Lackawanna Railroad main line, crossing the former Erie to Emporium line of the Pennsylvania Railroad at Maple Avenue in Corry on July 29, 1976. (Photograph by Kenneth C. Springirth.)

Consolidated Rail Corporation (still showing Penn Central Transportation Company markings) four-axle, 2,000-horsepower type GP38-2 locomotive No. 8132 is passing through Corry via the former Erie Lackawanna Railroad main line on July 29, 1976. (Photograph by Kenneth C. Springirth.)

On October 9, 1982, Consolidated Rail Corporation locomotives numbered 6459 and 6394 are powering a freight train over the former Erie Lackawanna Railroad main line, crossing East Pennsylvania Avenue at Corry. Both of these are 3,000-horsepower type SD40-2 locomotives built by the Electro-Motive Division of General Motors Corporation. (Photograph by Kenneth C. Springirth.)

The train for the inaugural run of the Northwest Pennsylvania Rail Authority is in Corry on former Erie Lackawanna Railroad trackage on September 7, 1996, headed by type GP38 locomotive No. 2001. Consolidated Rail Corporation had permission from the Interstate Commerce Commission to abandon the Corry to Meadville trackage during August 1994, and abandonment almost occurred until the agreement was finalized June 1997. (Photograph by Kenneth C. Springirth.)

Type FPA-2 locomotive No. 6758, built in 1955 for the Canadian National Railway by the Montreal Locomotive Works, is at Corry on the former main line of the Erie Lackawanna Railroad on September 4, 2000. The New York and Lake Erie Railroad (headquartered in Gowanda, New York, operates the Oil Creek and Titusville Railroad) acquired this locomotive along with No. 6764 in 1996. (Photograph by Kenneth C. Springirth.)

Western New York and Pennsylvania Railroad locomotive No. 421 is near Clark Road under the Smock Highway bridge in Meadville on February 4, 2010. This 2,400-horsepower type C424m (m denoting a rebuild) locomotive was built in 1963 by American Locomotive Company as No. 5206 for the Reading Railroad. It later served the Livonia, Avon, and Lakeville Railroad. (Photograph by Kenneth C. Springirth.)

Type C425 four-axle, 2,500-horsepower Western New York and Pennsylvania Railroad locomotive No. 4264 is at the railroad yard near Clark Road in Meadville on February 4, 2010. This locomotive was built in June 1966 by American Locomotive Company and had been used on a number of railroads, including the Pook Valley Rail System and the Massachusetts Central Railroad. (Photograph by Kenneth C. Springirth.)

On February 4, 2010, caboose No. C356 (owned by the Erie Lackawanna Historical Society) is displayed on the west side of the French Creek Parkway, south of the Mercer/Willow Street intersection in Meadville, by the French Creek Valley Railroad Historical Society. It was one of 20 cabooses, Nos. C351 to C370, built by the International Car Company in 1969 for the Erie Lackawanna Railway. The Erie Lackawanna Railway was formed April 1, 1968, as a subsidiary of Dereco, the holding company of the Norfolk and Western Railway. (Photograph by Kenneth C. Springirth.)

Five

KNOX AND KANE RAILROAD

The Knox and Kane Railroad operated from Knox in Clarion County via Kane to Mount Jewett in McKean County. It was constructed in several stages with a 3-foot narrow-gauge track between 1881 and 1883 by the Pittsburg and Western Railroad; the Pittsburgh, Bradford, and Buffalo Railroad; and the New York, Lake Erie, and Western Railroad. The Baltimore and Ohio Railroad operated the line as part of its Northern Subdivision beginning in 1902, and during 1911, most of the line was converted to the standard track gauge of 4-foot, 8.5-inches. It was purchased by the Knox and Kane Railroad from the Baltimore and Ohio Railroad in 1982.

It was a proud day for Mount Jewett, as 250 dignitaries and other people boarded the first excursion train in 28 years to cross the Kinzua Bridge on August 7, 1987. Knox and Kane Railroad president Sloan Cornell served as train engineer. Following a 30-minute train ride to the bridge, powered by steam locomotive No. 38, a ribbon-cutting ceremony took place. William C. Forrey, director of the Pennsylvania Bureau of State Parks, noted the sense of excitement at the site, commenting that, "Americans just like trains." The train crossed the bridge and made a return trip to Mount Jewett. Cornell spent about $1 million of his own money for the project and had a 35-year lease with the Pennsylvania Department of Environmental Resources for the use of the bridge. Hundreds of people lined up along both sides of the route at virtually every crossing from Mount Jewett to the Kinzua Bridge. The Knox and Kane Railroad began operating a 97-mile round-trip excursion from Marienville via Kane to the Kinzua Bridge using a steam locomotive from China with a 2-8-2 wheel arrangement and a Baldwin-built steam locomotive with a 2-8-0 wheel arrangement. On July 21, 2003, at 3:20 p.m. local time, a tornado struck the 301-foot-high, 2,053-foot-long Kinzua Bridge, collapsing 11 of the bridge's 20 towers. With the loss of the bridge, the railroad lost 75 percent of its passengers and ended excursion service during October 2004.

Construction of the first Kinzua Bridge is well underway in this 1882 scene. There was no scaffolding used in building the bridge. After the first tower was completed, a travelling crane was built to construct the towers. Phoenix Iron Works built the bridge using hollow iron tubes called "Phoenix Columns" at a cost of $167,000. (Scott Morgan collection.)

KINZUA BRIDGE BETWEEN BRADFORD AND KANE, PA. HEIGHT 301 FEET, LENGTH 2250 FEET.

One of Pennsylvania's most recognizable landmarks, the Kinzua Bridge is in this postcard dated July 9, 1917. The New York, Lake Erie, and Western Railroad had engineer Octave Chanute design the 301-foot-high and 2,053-foot-long wrought iron bridge, which was completed on August 29, 1882, at a cost of $167,000. It was rebuilt with steel at a cost of $275,000 and reopened September 25, 1900, to accommodate heavier trains.

This is a view of the Kinzua Bridge from the valley on July 7, 1963. In 1893, the New York, Lake Erie, and Western Railroad went bankrupt and merged with the Erie Railroad, which ended train service over this bridge on June 21, 1959. The state of Pennsylvania purchased the bridge and adjacent land and created Kinzua Bridge State Park, which was opened to the public in 1970. (Photograph by Kenneth C. Springirth.)

On June 14, 1948, Baltimore and Ohio Railroad class E-60a steam locomotive No. 3101, with a 2-8-0 wheel arrangement, and caboose No. C-1976 are at the Kane freight station. This was originally the narrow-gauge Pittsburg and Western Railroad, which was absorbed into the Baltimore and Ohio Railroad in 1911 and converted to standard gauge that year. The Pennsylvania Railroad line through Kane was south of this area. (Richard Bly collection.)

Baltimore and Ohio Railroad class E-60a steam locomotive No. 3102 with a 2-8-0 wheel arrangement is in Kane (roof sign on the building reads Kane Milling and Grocery Company) around 1920 with Biddle Street in downtown Kane on the other side of the buildings. The locomotive was originally Buffalo and Susquehanna Railroad locomotive No. 125. (Richard Bly collection.)

Baltimore and Ohio Railroad four-axle, 1,600-horsepower type AS-16 diesel locomotive No. 6213 is in Kane on September 7, 1963. This was one of 16 road switchers numbered 6200 to 6215 (originally numbered 890 to 905), built by Baldwin Locomotive Works for this railroad. (Photograph by Kenneth C. Springirth.)

Knox and Kane Railroad steam locomotive No. 38 is heading an excursion train that is reopening service to the Kinzua Bridge on August 7, 1987. This Consolidation-type locomotive with a 2-8-0 wheel arrangement was built by the Baldwin Locomotive Works originally for the Huntingdon and Broad Top Railroad in April 1927. (Photograph by Kenneth C. Springirth.)

On August 7, 1987, Knox and Kane Railroad locomotive No. 38 is powering a train for the Kinzua Bridge. The locomotive had 51-inch-diameter driver wheels, an empty weight of 163,730 pounds, and a tractive effort of 36,300 pounds. The Livonia, Avon, and Lakeville Railroad had restored this locomotive to service. It was later used on the Gettysburg Railroad. (Photograph by Kenneth C. Springirth.)

The Kinzua Bridge plays host to a Knox and Kane Railroad eight-car passenger train, powered by locomotive No. 38 on October 10, 1987. The Kinzua Bridge State Park had its official ribbon-cutting ceremony on July 5, 1975. The centerpiece in the park was the man-made Kinzua Bridge, which was the tallest bridge in the world until the 400-foot-high garabit viaduct, a railway arch bridge, was opened in France in 1885. (Photograph by Kenneth C. Springirth.)

With the trees changing colors, Knox and Kane Railroad locomotive No. 38 is leading the train across the Kinzua Bridge on October 10, 1987. The bridge was listed on the National Register of Historic Places on August 29, 1977, and on the National Register of Historic Civil Engineering Landmarks on June 26, 1982. (Photograph by Kenneth C. Springirth.)

Type GP9 diesel locomotive No. 14 is on the Knox and Kane Railroad on October 10, 1987. This locomotive was originally No. 39 on the Western Maryland Railroad, becoming No. 6414 on the Chessie System and No. 14 on the Knox and Kane Railroad. Later the locomotive was transferred to the Gettysburg Railroad but came back to the Knox and Kane Railroad as No. 39. (Photograph by Kenneth C. Springirth.)

On September 4, 2000, a variety of rolling stock is noted at the Knox and Kane Railroad yard in Marienville, including steam locomotive No. 58, a China Railways class SY steam locomotive built in July 1989, at the Tangshan Locomotive and Rolling Stock Works. The locomotive was heavily damaged in a fire on March 16, 2008, and was purchased by the Valley Railroad for restoration. (Photograph by Kenneth C. Springirth.)

A Knox and Kane Railroad caboose is at the end of a train in Marienville on September 4, 2000. For the 97-mile round-trip excursion, the train left Marienville at 8:30 a.m. and stopped at Kane at 10:30 a.m., where passengers could board for the shorter 32-mile round-trip to the Kinzua Bridge. (Photograph by Kenneth C. Springirth.)

A Knox and Kane Railroad excursion train is crossing forest road 133 near the Kane station on August 29, 2003. On July 21, 2003, a tornado with winds of up to 94 miles per hour struck the Kinzua Bridge and in less than 30 seconds caused 11 of the 20 bridge towers to fall with damage occurring upon impact with the ground. The railroad excursion service continued to operate to the bridge but not on the bridge. (Photograph by Kenneth C. Springirth.)

After a short stop in Kane to pickup passengers, the Knox and Kane Railroad train prepares to continue the final leg of the journey to the Kinzua Bridge on August 29, 2003. For the first few miles east of Kane, the railroad was south of U.S. Highway 6. The loss of the Kinzua Bridge resulted in a severe ridership decline for the excursion service. (Photograph by Kenneth C. Springirth.)

East of Kane, the Knox and Kane Railroad locomotive No. 39 leads the mixed train of freight and passenger cars across U.S. Highway 6 on August 29, 2003. The railroad was then north of U.S. Highway 6 until Mount Jewett, where it veered north to the Kinzua Bridge. (Photograph by Kenneth C. Springirth.)

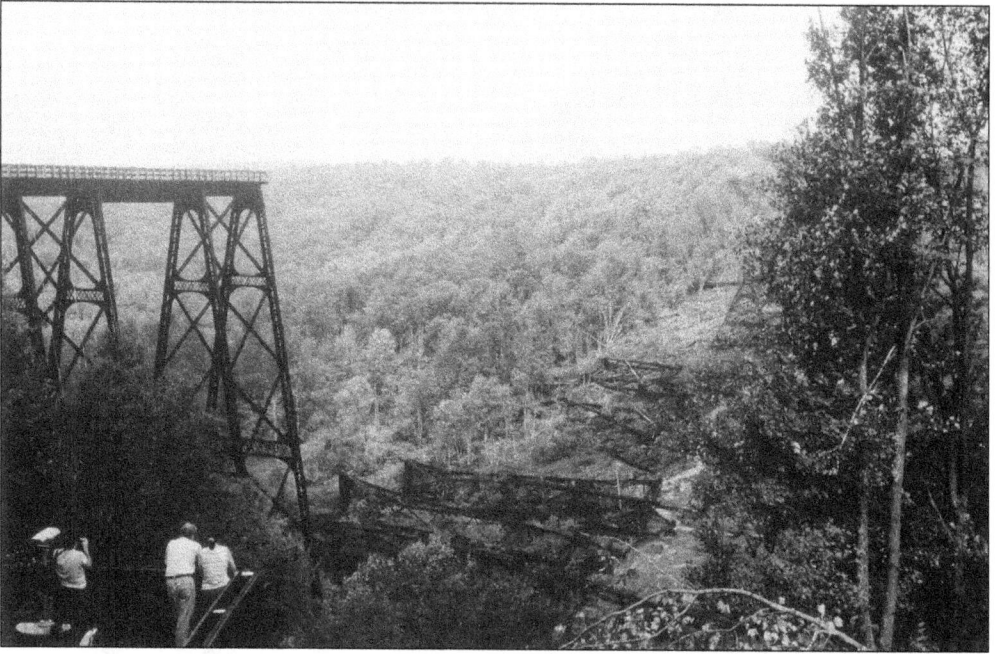

On August 29, 2003, the remains of the Kinzua Bridge are in view at the observation area at the Kinzua Bridge State Park. Corrosion of the base bolts holding the bases of the towers to the foundation was a major factor in the bridge failure from the July 21, 2003, tornado that caused 11 of the 20 bridge towers to fall. (Photograph by Kenneth C. Springirth.)

A Knox and Kane Railroad passenger train arrives at the Kinzua Bridge State Park on August 29, 2003. With the train no longer able to cross the bridge, ridership declined, and excursion service ended during October 2004. No local or overhead freight traffic has moved over the line since the first quarter of 2006. (Photograph by Kenneth C. Springirth.)

Six

REGIONAL AND SHORTLINE RAILROADS

Starting July 21, 1903, as the Brookville and Mahoning Railroad, the line opened from Brookville to Brockway in 1908, and by 1909, it became the Pittsburg and Shawmut Railroad. At that time, Pittsburgh was spelled without the "h." Genesee and Wyoming, Inc., acquired it during 1996. The Tionesta Valley Railway was chartered on September 9, 1879, and completed a 13-mile line from Sheffield to Sheffield Junction on September 19, 1882. Sheffield Junction was reached by the Pittsburg and Western Railroad in October 1882. Basically a lumber railroad, the Depression drastically reduced revenues, and the Tionesta Valley Railway was abandoned in June 1942.

The Wellsville, Addison, and Galeton Railroad was formed in 1954 to operate about 91 miles of the Baltimore and Ohio Railroad track consisting of a line from Galeton to Wellsville, New York, and another line from Galeton to Addison, New York. The Buffalo and Susquehanna Railroad, created in 1893, originally operated this trackage and by 1905 was extended southwest to the coal mining area of Sagamore, Pennsylvania. The Wellsville, Addison, and Galeton Railroad became known as the "Sole Leather Line" in reference to the large number of tanneries it served. It was abandoned on March 13, 1979.

On October 17, 1907, the East Erie Commercial Railroad was incorporated to provide switching and terminal services for Erie area businesses and industries. In 1980, the railroad had 12.64 miles of track, including a test track with six different gauges ranging from 24 inches to 5-foot, 6 inches and was electrified with both a catenary and third rail to test locomotives built at the General Electric Company plant in Erie.

What ultimately became the Bessemer and Lake Erie Railroad expanded northward reaching Albion on June 8, 1891. The railroad continued northward to Girard and obtained trackage rights over the New York, Chicago, and St. Louis Railroad (Nickel Plate Road) to Erie. On August 15, 1892, the railroad completed its line from Albion to Conneaut, Ohio. In Erie, the line was completed to Twelfth Street near Peach Street on May 29, 1893. The Bessemer and Lake Erie Railroad ended all passenger service with the last run from Erie to Greenville on March 5, 1955. Canadian National Railway acquired the railroad on May 10, 2004.

Bradford, Bordell, and Kinzua Railroad locomotive No. 10, with a freight train, is shown in this postcard dated October 4, 1909. This Mogul type locomotive with a 2-6-0 wheel arrangement and 42-inch-diameter driver wheels was built by Baldwin Locomotive Works and was designed for slow, heavy freight service.

A passenger train is shown on the narrow-gauge Bradford, Bordell, and Kinzua Railroad in this postcard dated September 3, 1907. The September 25, 1881, schedule showed four trains in each direction from Bradford to Smethport, Monday to Saturday, and two trains in each direction on Sunday. Much of the area traversed by the railroad was sparsely settled.

A Big Level and Kinzua Railroad train is at Biddle Street in Kane in this postcard postmarked September 30, 1908. In 1886, the Big Level and Kinzua Railroad was leased to the Bradford, Bordell, and Kinzua Railroad. On December 11, 1903, the Buffalo and Susquehanna Railroad purchased the Bradford, Bordell, and Kinzua, and on January 4, 1904, it became the Buffalo, Bradford, and Kane Railroad. (Richard Bly collection.)

A mixed train of the narrow-gauge Bradford, Bordell, and Kinzua Railroad (which on January 4, 1904, became the Buffalo, Bradford, and Kane Railroad) is at Mount Jewett in this postcard dated 1913. This railroad operated its last scheduled passenger train from Bradford to Kane on September 2, 1906. The two tracks in the lower portion of the picture are the standard-gauge Buffalo, Rochester, and Pittsburgh Railway. This line linked Rochester, New York, with the coal fields of central Pennsylvania. It became part of the Baltimore and Ohio Railroad on January 1, 1932. (Gerald N. D'Aurora collection.)

Narrow-gauge Bradford, Bordell, and Kinzua Railroad engine No. 6 is shown hauling engine No. 14 on a transfer truck crossing the standard-gauge Pittsburg, Shawmut, and Northern Railroad at Smethport around 1910. Elisha K. Kane owned the narrow-gauge transfer car. With the third rail, the transfer car could accommodate narrow- and standard-gauge cars. Plans were made to convert this line to standard gauge, but it took a court case to resolve it. (Scott Morgan collection.)

In this 1910 scene, a standard-gauge tank car is on the transfer car being pulled across the standard-gauge Pittsburg, Shawmut, and Northern Railroad at Smethport by narrow-gauge Bradford, Bordell, and Kinzua Railroad engine No. 6. In 1913, the court ruled this line could be converted to standard gauge. This was accomplished. The transfer car and narrow-gauge locomotive were scrapped. (Scott Morgan collection.)

Loop De Loop, P. S. & N. R. R., North of Saint Mary's, Pa.

A Pittsburg, Shawmut, and Northern Railroad train is negotiating the Kasson loop north of Clermont around 1909. The railroad climbed 525 feet to reach the Big Level plateau, and a giant hairpin loop was built, which increased the mileage by 2.5 miles at an acceptable grade of 1.3 percent. Passenger service on the loop began on October 25, 1903. The line was abandoned in 1947. (Gerald N. D'Aurora collection.)

Around 1900, a Pittsburg, Shawmut, and Northern Railroad train is at Clermont, which is east of Kane. Clermont became a boomtown when the Buffalo Coal Company expanded their mining operations. The coal mines were later abandoned, the population declined, and the railroad ceased operation on April 1, 1947. (Kane Historic Preservation Society collection.)

THE PITTSBURG, SHAWMUT & NORTHERN R. R. CO.

BETWEEN ST. MARYS, BROOKVILLE, RAMSAYTOWN, KITTANNING, FORD CITY AND CADOGAN.

Southward				Mls.	STATIONS	Northward				
*17	*3	*15	*1			*2	*16	*4	*6	*18
PM	PM	AM	AM			AM	AM	PM	PM	PM
....	2.45	....	7.30	0	Lv... St. Marys ...Ar	11.00	....	....	4.55	....
....	f2.52	....	7.37	1	....Kaulmont......	10.52	....	....	f4.47	....
....	f2.58	....	f 7.43	4	....Detsch......	10.45	....	....	f4.41	....
....	f	....	f	5	....Seheberel......	f	....	....	f	....
....	f	....	f	7	....Gillen......	f	....	....	f	....
....	3.10	....	7.56	8	....Paine......	10.32	....	....	4.27	....
....	3.14	....	8.00	10	....Kersey......	10.28	....	....	4.22	....
....	3.18	....	8.04	11	....Dagus......	10.25	....	....	4.19	....
....	f3.25	....	f 8.11	14	....Shelvey......	10.18	....	....	f4.12	....
....	f	....	f	15	....Cuneo......	f	....	....	f	....
....	f3.40	....	f 8.26	19	....Brandy Camp......	10.03	....	....	f3.57	....
....	f	....	f	20	....Elbon......	f	....	....	f	....
....	3.50	....	8.34	21	....Hyde......	9.56	....	....	3.50	....
....	f3.53	....	f 8.37	22	....Helen Mills......	f9.52	....	....	3.47	....
....	3.55	....	8.42	24	Ar....Brockport...Lv	9.47	....	....	3.42	....
....	4.07	....	8.52	26	Ar....Shawmut......	9.37	....	....	3.33	....
....	....	....	8.57	27	Lv....Drummond ...Lv	....	....	....	3.29	....
....	4.07	....	9.01	26	Lv ....Shawmut...Ar	9.37	....	....	3.25	....
....	4.16	....	9.10	24	Lv....Brockport...Ar	9.28	....	....	3.16	....
....	4.24	....	9.18	25	....Keystone......	9.18	....	....	3.08	....
....	4.30	....	9.26	26	....Crenshaw......	9.11	....	....	3.01	....
....	f4.38	....	f 9.34	28	..Brockwayville (Erie Station)	f9.03	....	....	f2.53	....
....	f	....	f	28	..Brockwayville (P.S. & N. Station).	f	....	....	f	....
....	f	....	f	31	....Smith Summit ...	f	....	....	f	....
....	f4.46	....	f 9.44	34	....Beughtin......	f8.53	....	....	f2.44	....
....	f	....	f	35	....Sugar Hill......	f	....	....	f	....
....	f	....	f	36	....Relts......	f	....	....	f	....
....	4.57	....	9.55	37	....Allen......	8.41	....	....	2.35	....
....	f5.05	....	f10.03	40	....North Sulger......	f8.33	....	....	f2.25	....
....	f	....	f	42	....Sulger......	f	....	....	f	....
....	f	....	f	44	....South Sulger...	f	....	....	f	....
....	f5.19	....	f10.19	47	....Port Barnett...	f8.20	....	....	f2.09	....
5.35	5.24	6.20	10.27	48	Ar Lv ....Brookville... Lv Ar	8.15	10.50	11.40	2.05 6.35	3 15
5.46	5.34	6.30	11.10	51	Ar Lv ....Norman ... Lv Ar	....	10.40	11.29	5.23	8 06
5.45	5.39	6.34	11.15	53	....Colon	....	10.36	11.25	5.49	8 02
....	5.44	....	11.20	54	Ar.. Ramsaytown... Lv	....	10.31	11.20	5.44	....
f5.53	f6.38	....	....	55	....Tait......	....	10.31	....	....	f7 58
5.58	6 43	....	....	56	..Knoxdale (Main Line) ...	....	10 26	....	....	7 54
f6.04	f6 49	....	....	59	....Indian Camp	....	10.19	....	....	f7 49
f	f	....	....	61	....East Branch......	....	f	....	....	f
f6.13	f6 59	....	....	64	....Coulter......	....	10.08	....	....	f7 39
f6.17	f7.03	....	....	65	....Sprankle Mills ...	....	10.03	....	....	f7.35
f	f	....	....	67	....Mauk	....	f	....	....	f
f6.26	f7.11	....	....	69	....Dora......	....	f9.52	....	....	f7 25
f	f	....	....	72	....Ringgold......	....	f	....	....	f
6.31	7.16	....	....	75	....Timblin......	....	9.46	....	....	7 19
f6.37	f7.26	....	....	77	....McWilliams......	....	f9.38	....	....	f7 11
f6.42	f7.30	....	....	80	....Eddyville......	....	f9 33	....	....	f7 06
6.49	7.42	....	....	81	....Putneyville......	....	9 25	....	....	6 58
6.54	7.42	....	....	83	....Oakland Jct.......	....	9 21	....	....	6 54
f6.58	f7.46	....	....	87	....Colwell Cut......	....	f9.16	....	....	f6 50
7.08	8.00	....	....	90	Ar....Tidal Jct....... Lv	....	9 05	....	....	6 40
f7 14	f8.14	f	*31	91	Ar....Mahoning ...Av	....	f8 58	....	*32	f6 33
f	....	PM	f		....Freidenheim......	AM	f	....	PM	f
f7.21	....	f8.14	....		....West Templeton ...	....	f8 49	....	....	f6 25
7.27	....	f8 20	....	95	....Dickey......	....	f8 43	....	....	6 19
f7.30	....	8 36	....	96	Ar Lv ..Bridgeburg (See Note 1, Page 6.) .. Ar Lv	....	8 36 8 13	....	....	f6.16
....	....	....	....	97	....Tarrtown......	....	....	....	....	....
f7 33	5.15	f8.40	7 10	98	....Furnace Run......	6.55	f8.06	....	5.05	f6 12
....	f	....	f	99	....Mohawk......	....	f	....	....	f
7.40	5.25	8 47	7.20	100	....Kittanning......	6.45	8 0.	....	4 55	6 05
....	5.38	....	7.33	104	....Ford City......	....	7.45	....	....	5.50
....	5.44	....	7.39	106	Ar....Cadogan...Lv	....	7.39	....	....	5.44
PM	PM	AM	AM			AM	AM	PM	PM	PM

* Daily Except Sunday.   f Flag station.   Trains stop on signal.

4

THE PITTSBURG, SHAWMUT & NORTHERN R. R. CO.

Hazelhurst Branch

Southward		Mls.	STATIONS	Northward	
*317	*311			*312	*318
PM	PM			PM	PM
8.20	1.06	0	Lv.... Kasson ... Ar	1 30	8.44
f 8.24	f 1.10	2	....Marvindale ...	f 1.26	f 8.39
8.31	1.19	5	Ar....Hazelhurst...Lv	1 19	8.31
PM	PM			PM	PM

Byrnedale Branch

Southward		Mls.	STATIONS	Northward	
*303	*301			*300	*302
PM	AM			AM	PM
2.45	7.30	0	Lv... St. Marys ... Ar	11.00	4.55
4.35	8.00	9	....Paine	7.48	4.16
....	....	10	....Dollinger ...	....	....
5.08	8.55	17	....Byrnedale ...	6.48	3.25
5.16	9.10	19	....Weedville ...	6.38	3.10
5.25	9.30	20	Ar.....Force Lv	6.30	3.00
....	....	21	....Cardiff ...	....	....
PM	AM			AM	PM

Conifer Branch

Southward		Mls.	STATIONS	Northward	
*325	*323			*324	*326
PM	AM			AM	PM
5.24	10.27	0	Lv... Brookville ... Ar	11.40	6.35
5.34	10.40	4	Ar Lv Norman {	11.29	6.23
5.04	10.40	5		11.10	6.22
f	f	6	....Hunts Run...	f	f
f 6.00	f10.46	6	....Stanton ...	f11.03	f 6.16
f	f	7	....McGareys...	f	f
6.08	10.54	8	Ar.....Conifer ...Lv	10.54	6.08
PM	AM			AM	PM

Between Seminole and Chickasaw

Southward				Mls.	STATIONS	Northward				
*352 *353	*350	*346 *347	*344			*342 *343	*345	*348 *349	*351	
PM	PM	AM	AM			AM	AM	PM	PM	
7.07	6 35	9.34	7.27	0	Lv.....Seminole ... Ar	7.27	9 34	6 35	7 07	
7 21	6.50	9.48	7.41	3	....Oakland Jct......	7.15	9.22	6.15	6 55	
....	....	....	....	5	....Colwell Cut ...	....	....	....	....	
....	....	....	....	8	....Reedy......	....	....	....	....	
7.43	....	10.12	....	9	....Tidal Jct.......	6.50	....	6.05	....	
7.55	....	10.25	....	12	Ar....Chickasaw ...Lv	6.35	....	5.30	....	
PM		AM	AM			AM	AM	PM	PM	

Clarion River Division

Southward				Mls.	STATIONS	Northward				
*337	*355	*353	*331			*330	*332	*334	*336	
PM	PM	AM	AM			AM	AM	PM	PM	
6.00	3.40	9.35	7.25	0	Lv....Croyland ...Ar	7 15	9.05	3.14	5.48	
6.05	4.05	10.05	7.30	1	....Carman	7.10	8.59	3.06	5.44	
6.10	....	10.10	....	2	Ar Lv Portland Mills {	7.05	8.54	3.00	5.39	
f 4.17	....	....	....	4	....Bear Creek ...	....	f 8.49	....	....	
4.31	....	11.06	7.54	7	....Arroyo	....	8.35	2.22	5.20	
....	....	....	....	10	....Irwintown	....	....	....	....	
4.51	....	11.30	8.14	12	Ar....Hallton ...Lv	....	8.14	2.00	5.00	
PM		AM	AM			AM	AM	PM	PM	

Daily Except Sunday.   f Flag station.   Trains stop on signal.

5

The Pittsburg, Shawmut, and Northern Railroad schedule, effective November 7, 1915, shows two trains in each direction from St. Marys via Brookville to Ramsaytown. In addition, there were two trains in each direction from Brookville to Kittanning and two trains in each direction from Furnace Run via Kittanning to Cadogan. There was also passenger service on many of the branch lines. All of the passenger trains were daily except Sunday.

A Pittsburg and Shawmut Railroad steam locomotive is at the borough of West Kittanning with the Allegheny River in view in this postcard dated October 3, 1920. In 1936, the railroad had a daily, except Sunday, train from Timblin via West Kittanning to Glen Irwin, and there was an additional train from Furnace Run to Glen Irwin.

Two 1,200-horsepower type SW9 diesel switchers, Nos. 233 and 231, built by the Electro-Motive Division of General Motors Corporation, are at the borough of Kittanning ready to assist a steam excursion on the Pittsburg and Shawmut Railroad on October 14, 1973. The railroad had nine of these switchers numbered 231 to 239. (Photograph by Kenneth C. Springirth.)

Kittanning is the starting point for a steam locomotive excursion on the Pittsburg and Shawmut Railroad to the borough of Brookville on October 14, 1973. This was former Reading Railroad class T-1 steam locomotive No. 2102 with a 4-8-4 wheel arrangement, renumbered as 302, and relettered for the Delaware and Hudson Railroad sesquicentennial in 1973. (Photograph by Kenneth C. Springirth.)

Pittsburg and Shawmut Railroad 1,200-horsepower type SW9 diesel switcher No. 232 is at the main shops in Brookville on October 14, 1973. The 88-mile main line of the railroad was from the borough of Brockway to the borough of Freeport. Since January 1, 2004, it has been operated as part of the Buffalo and Pittsburgh Railroad. (Photograph by Kenneth C. Springirth.)

Tionesta Valley Railway locomotive No. 1, built by Brooks Locomotive Works in 1882 with a 4-4-0 wheel arrangement, is powering a two-car passenger train at the Pennsylvania Railroad depot in Sheffield. Passenger service operated from Sheffield to Sheffield Junction where connections were made with the Pittsburg and Western Railroad. The locomotive was scrapped in 1935. (Sheffield Depot Preservation Society, Inc.)

Two vintage Tionesta Valley Railway passenger cars are waiting for the next assignment. On June 30, 1917, the railroad had 16 locomotives, 556 freight cars, and 4 passenger cars. In 1895, the railroad built a number of branch lines to serve tanneries and sawmills. From 1918 to 1930, the railroad handled a large volume of lumber and other freight with a significant amount of freight transferred to the Pennsylvania Railroad at Sheffield. (Sheffield Depot Preservation Society, Inc.)

Built in 1920 by Heisler Locomotive Works, Tionesta Valley Railway locomotive No. 16 is in Sheffield. The locomotive featured two cylinders on a 45-degree angle. Power went to a longitudinal drive shaft that drove the outboard axle on each powered truck. The inboard axle of each truck was driven from the outboard one by external side rods. (Sheffield Depot Preservation Society, Inc.)

Tionesta Valley Railway locomotive No. 16 is at the east branch lumbering section near the community of Nebraska in the summer of 1937. The Central Pennsylvania Lumber Company opened a new sawmill in Sheffield in February 1908 and sidings to the lumber yards had a third rail installed to allow the use of both standard- and narrow-gauge cars and locomotives. (Photograph by Louis B. Jones.)

Locomotive No. 10, built by Brooks Locomotive Works in 1904 with a 2-6-0 wheel arrangement, is at the Tionesta Valley Railway yard at Sheffield in the late 1930s. After 1936, only the 13-mile line from Sheffield to Sheffield Junction remained in operation. After receiving permission to abandon the line, trackage was removed in June 1942. (Sheffield Depot Preservation Society, Inc.)

Otto Chemical Company saddleback locomotive with a 0-4-0T wheel arrangement built by Davenport Locomotive Works is at work at the plant in the township of Sergeant on July 7, 1963. "T" denotes the tank locomotive that carries its own fuel and water on it instead of pulling it behind in a tender. This was the last vintage locomotive of its type operating in northwestern Pennsylvania moving small cars of chemical wood, and the plant was later closed. (Photograph by Kenneth C. Springirth.)

An open summer trolley car of the DuBois Traction Company is providing a convenient connection to the Buffalo Rochester and Pittsburgh Railway at the city of DuBois in this postcard postmarked July 11, 1911. Trolley car service began in DuBois on October 17, 1891, and ended August 5, 1926. At its peak, there was trolley car service from DuBois to Big Run.

The Buffalo, Rochester, and Pittsburgh Railway station in the borough of Punxsutawney is a busy place in this postcard dated February 3, 1912. The May 28, 1916, schedule showed six passenger trains in each direction, Monday through Saturday (four on Sunday in each direction), stopping at Punxsutawney, of which two trains in each direction operated daily from Buffalo to Pittsburgh. The railroad was noted for its attractive passenger stations.

8086. B. R. & P. Depot, Ridgway, Pa.

The attractive Buffalo, Rochester, and Pittsburgh Railway station in the borough of Ridgway is an example of the railroad's facilities, seen in this postcard dated 1912. According to the May 28, 1916, timetable, four passenger trains in each direction, Monday through Saturday (three southbound and two northbound on Sunday), stopped at this station. Three of the southbound trains and two of the northbound trains were daily through trains from Buffalo to Pittsburgh. (Gerald N. D'Aurora collection.)

Depot, Coudersport, Pa.

Passengers are waiting for the Coudersport and Port Allegany Railroad train at the impressive brick and stone station built in 1899 in the borough of Coudersport. The railroad was opened from Coudersport to Port Allegany on October 1, 1882. It was purchased by the H. E. Salzberg Company in 1964 and became part of the Wellsville Addison and Galeton Railroad. Permission was received on December 8, 1970, to abandon the line. (Gerald N. D'Aurora collection.)

111

The 660-horsepower East Erie Commercial Railroad diesel locomotive No. 20, in its safety red with federal yellow lettering and trim paint scheme, is handling a special excursion train for Interrail 77, the International Railfans and Rail Modeler's Meet on April 30, 1977, on the General Electric Company 4-mile test track in Harborcreek Township, which is normally used to test locomotives. (Photograph by Kenneth C. Springirth.)

On April 30, 1977, the Lake Shore Railway Historical Society, Inc., observation car, "Central Park," is on the Interrail 77 excursion train on the General Electric Company test track in Lawrence Park Township. The International Railfans and Rail Modeler's Meet was hosted by the Lake Shore Railway Historical Society, Inc., and North East Model Railroad Association for the Niagara Frontier Region National Model Railroader Association Spring Convention. (Photograph by Kenneth C. Springirth.)

Wellsville, Addison, and Galeton Railroad 125-ton center cab diesels Nos. 1300 and 1200 are at the railroad's shops in the borough of Galeton on July 16, 1966. The railroad also had five 132-ton center cab diesels. The General Electric Company built these seven diesel locomotives originally for the Ford Motor Company. (Photograph by Kenneth C. Springirth.)

On July 16, 1966, the Wellsville, Addison, and Galeton Railroad caboose No. C2620 is at the shops in Galeton. Flooding caused major damage, and loss of traffic resulted in the railroad filing for abandonment in 1975. The Interstate Commerce Commission approved the abandonment in 1978, and the last freight ran on March 13, 1979. (Photograph by Kenneth C. Springirth.)

BUFFALO & SUSQUEHANNA R. R. DEPOT, DUBOIS, PA.

In this postcard dated 1909, a Buffalo and Susquehanna Railroad passenger train has arrived at the DuBois station. The railroad operated from Addison, New York, via Galeton and DuBois to Sagamore, Pennsylvania. There was also a line from Galeton to Buffalo, New York. The Baltimore and Ohio Railroad purchased the railroad in 1932. A portion later became the Wellsville, Addison, and Galeton Railroad. (Gerald N. D'Aurora collection.)

Platform Station B. & L.E. Railraod, Osgood, Pa.

A few people are at the village of Osgood station of the Bessemer and Lake Erie Railroad for the southbound train to Greenville. The June 4, 1916, schedule showed four southbound (two on Sunday) and four northbound (two on Sunday) passenger trains stopping in Osgood. (Gerald N. D'Aurora collection.)

114

On the Bissemer near Greenville, Pa.

A southbound Bessemer and Lake Erie Railroad freight train is on the high level bridge in Osgood in this scene around 1908. Bessemer was spelled incorrectly on the postcard. This 8.81-mile bypass route around Greenville was constructed in 1901 from the village of Kremis to the village of Osgood and became known as the K-O cutoff. (Gerald N. D'Aurora collection.)

P. B. & L. E. Station, Mercer, Pa.

Crowds of well-dressed men are at the Pittsburg, Bessemer, and Lake Erie Railroad station in the borough of Mercer in this postcard dated 1909. The postcard was out of date because on December 31, 1900, the railroad became the Bessemer and Lake Erie Railroad. The June 4, 1916, schedule showed service from Erie via Mercer to Butler and East Pittsburgh. (Gerald N. D'Aurora collection.)

Passengers from the National Biscuit plant in Pittsburgh have arrived via the Bessemer and Lake Erie Railroad to Conneaut Lake Park. There was railroad passenger service from East Pittsburgh via Butler to Conneaut Lake Park. On the weekends, as many as 16 special passenger trains a day operated to Conneaut Lake Park. (Gerald N. D'Aurora collection.)

A Bessemer and Lake Erie Railroad passenger train is ready to board passengers at the borough of Conneautville in this postcard dated 1912. The June 4, 1916, schedule for Monday through Saturday showed three southbound trains (two on Sunday) from Erie to Butler and three northbound trains (two on Sunday) from Butler to Erie. (Gerald N. D'Aurora collection.)

B. & L. E. Round House, Albion, Pa.

Steam locomotive No. 141 (a class C1F with a 2-8-0 wheel arrangement built by American Locomotive Company of Pittsburgh during 1909) is on the turntable with No. 78 (a class C1B built by Pittsburgh Locomotive Works during 1899) in the background at the Bessemer and Lake Erie Railroad roundhouse at the borough of Albion in this postcard dated 1918. Both locomotives had a 2-8-0 wheel arrangement. (Gerald N. D'Aurora collection.)

An air view of the Bessemer and Lake Erie Railroad roundhouse and yard in Albion shows this was an important facility. With a poor economy, the July 6, 1983, *Erie Morning News* reported that "the once busy Bessemer and Lake Erie Railroad terminal in Albion will soon be nothing more than a minor rail station." (Gerald N. D'Aurora collection.)

117

Bessemer and Lake Railroad locomotive No. 150 is leaving the yards in Conneaut, Ohio, around 1920 to deliver the hopper cars of iron ore to the steel mills of Pittsburgh. The class C3A locomotive, with a 2-8-0 wheel arrangement and 54-inch-diameter driver wheels, was built during 1900 by Pittsburgh Locomotive Works.

On October 27, 1963, Bessemer and Lake Erie Railroad diesel locomotive No. 853 is heading a freight train passing through the borough of Cranesville. This was one of seven 1,800-horsepower type SD18 locomotives, numbered 851 to 857, built for this railroad by the Electro-Motive Division of General Motors Corporation in January 1963. (Photograph by Kenneth C. Springirth.)

Seven

OIL CREEK AND TITUSVILLE RAILROAD

Following the February 1, 1968, merger of the Pennsylvania Railroad and the New York Central Railroad, through freight traffic from Pittsburgh via Oil City and Titusville was rerouted via Youngstown and Ashtabula, Ohio. After Consolidated Rail Corporation took over on April 1, 1976, freight traffic from Rynd Farm to Titusville became occasional. On November 30, 1981, Consolidated Rail Corporation announced it planned to abandon 15.3 miles of track from Titusville to Rouseville, because it was no longer profitable. In 1982, the track to Titusville was kept open to service the 2.5-mile Fieldmore Springs line, which ran from Titusville to East Titusville. The August 18, 1983, *Titusville Herald* reported, "Yesterday (August 17, 1983), what may be the last train to enter or leave the city (Titusville), made its appearance." The train's cargo was two hopper cars, each loaded with 180,000 pounds of plastic pellets for Oil Creek Plastics, Inc., of East Titusville. Local people in Titusville and Oil City formed the Oil Creek Railway Historical Society and purchased the line for $286,000. Passenger and freight service was then operated by the Oil Creek and Titusville Railroad, which is affiliated with the New York and Lake Erie Railroad.

Passenger excursion service on the Oil Creek and Titusville Railroad began on July 18, 1986, using passenger cars leased from a number of different sources operating through Oil Creek State Park, where oil was discovered and literally changed the world. Seven electric-powered, multiple-unit commuter cars, each seating 76 (built by the Pullman Company in 1930 and used in Hoboken, New Jersey, commuter service until 1986) were purchased from the Delaware, Lackawanna, and Western Railroad. The cars were reconditioned and placed in service during 1987 with each car named for an individual that played an important role in the development of the oil industry. Following extensive renovations, the Perry Street station in Titusville was opened along with stations at Drake Well, Petroleum Centre, and Rynd Farm, which is the southern terminus of the line. Freight service was provided on a 2.5-mile section of the Fieldmore Springs branch from East Titusville to Titusville of the former New York Central Railroad line that was once the Dunkirk, Allegheny Valley, and Pittsburgh Railroad.

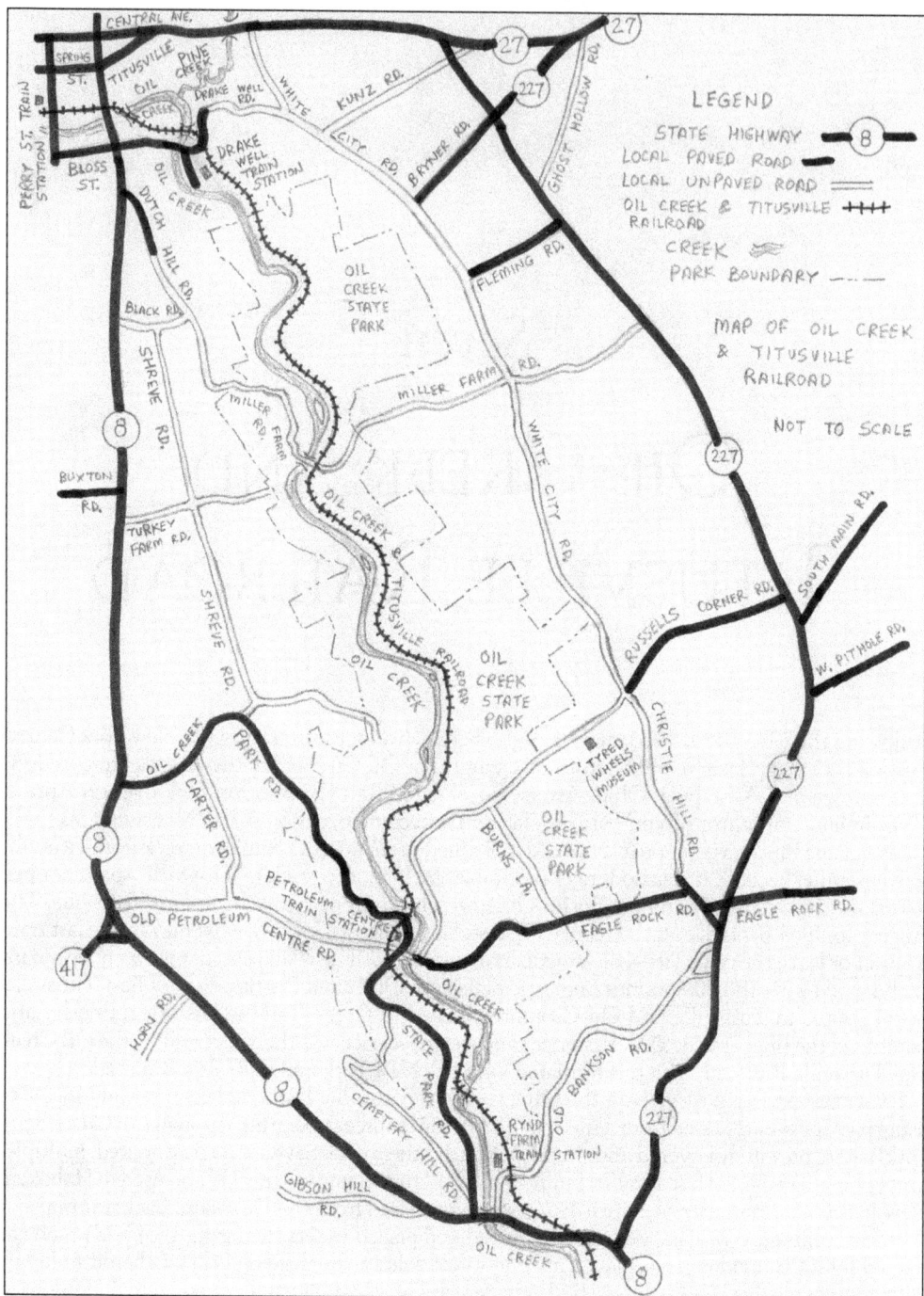

As shown by the map, the Oil Creek and Titusville Railroad operates from Perry Street station in Titusville through Oil Creek State Park to Rynd Farm, with stations at Drake Well and Petroleum Centre. It was along Oil Creek, just south of Titusville, that oil was discovered on August 27, 1859. It marked the beginning of a new industry. Thousands of people came into the valley in search of oil. When production declined by 1873, nature began to slowly reclaim the area so that today the valley has tree coverage almost like it was before the oil boom took place.

On July 6, 2008, an Oil Creek and Titusville Railroad excursion train pulls out of Perry Street station in Titusville using 2,000-horsepower type M420W diesel locomotive No. 3568. This locomotive was built by Montreal Locomotive Works of Montreal, Quebec, Canada, originally for the Canadian National Railway in 1977 and was later used on the St. Thomas and Eastern Railway. (Photograph by Kenneth C. Springirth.)

Oil Creek and Titusville Railroad 1,000-horsepower type S-2 diesel locomotive No. 85 is on the siding near Perry Street in Titusville on June 21, 2008. American Locomotive Company built the locomotive in 1950, and it was purchased by the Oil Creek Railway Historical Society in 1999. (Photograph by Kenneth C. Springirth.)

A southbound Oil Creek and Titusville Railroad train powered by locomotive No. 3568 traverses Oil Creek State Park on its way to Rynd Farm on July 6, 2008. The 7,096-acre park in Venango County features picturesque Oil Creek meandering through the Oil Creek Gorge that was formed during the ice age when a huge volume of water breached an area and eroded a deep gorge. (Photograph by Kenneth C. Springirth.)

On July 6, 2008, at Rynd Farm, Oil Creek and Titusville Railroad locomotive No. 3568 is switching a freight car that had been delivered at the borough of Rouseville. This is an interchange point with the Western New York and Pennsylvania Railroad, which leases trackage from the Norfolk Southern Railway from Rouseville via Oil City and Franklin to Meadville. (Photograph by Kenneth C. Springirth.)

Northbound locomotive No. 3568 is nearing Drake Well station with an Oil Creek and Titusville Railroad passenger train on July 6, 2008. Following the decline in oil production, the trees in the hills and valleys were cut for the lumber industry. During the Great Depression, the Civilian Conservation Corps cleaned the area and replanted the trees. (Photograph by Kenneth C. Springirth.)

On July 6, 2008, Oil Creek and Titusville Railroad locomotive No. 3568 is powering a train crossing Oil Creek on the northbound trip to Titusville. Passenger car No. 59 (second car behind the locomotive) was named for Edwin L. Drake who supervised the drilling of the first successful oil well by William A. Smith on August 27, 1859. (Photograph by Kenneth C. Springirth.)

Oil Creek and Titusville Railroad 1,000-horsepower type S-2 locomotive No. 75, built by American Locomotive Company in 1947 (leased from the New York and Lake Erie Railroad), is crossing Oil Creek on a southbound run to Rynd Farm on October 11, 2009. Oil Creek is crossed four times on the run from Titusville to Rynd Farm. (Photograph by Kenneth C. Springirth.)

Rynd Farm is the scene for Oil Creek and Titusville Railroad locomotive No. 75 as it prepares to move a tank car to the front of the passenger train for the trip north to Titusville on October 17, 2009. This interchange point with the Western New York and Pennsylvania Railroad gives Titusville a connection with the nation's rail system. (Photograph by Kenneth C. Springirth.)

Amid the picturesque trees in their autumn colors, Oil Creek and Titusville Railroad locomotive No. 75 is leading the train northward nearing Petroleum Centre station on October 11, 2009. This area was booming with oil wells from 1863 to 1870. There were hotels, commercial establishments, and machine shops. With a decline in oil production by 1873, the town soon became deserted. (Photograph by Kenneth C. Springirth.)

On October 18, 2009, Drake Well station is the location for the display of a vintage flat car that was used to haul oil. On September 1, 1865, Amos and James Densmore placed two wooden tanks on a flat railway car for shipping crude oil. Their idea was successful, and the car became known as a "Densmore" car. An Oil Creek and Titusville Railroad passenger train in the background has stopped at the station. (Photograph by Kenneth C. Springirth.)

A southbound Oil Creek and Titusville Railroad train, powered by locomotive No. 75, is passing Petroleum Centre station on October 17, 2009. There is a visitor's center at the Petroleum Centre train station that features historical displays. Following the August 27, 1859, discovery of oil, Petroleum Centre rapidly expanded to a population of 3,000 by 1863 but quickly declined when oil production declined. (Photograph by Kenneth C. Springirth.)

The Oil Creek and Titusville Railroad passenger train, headed by locomotive No. 75, has just crossed Franklin Street in Titusville on October 25, 2009, for a southbound run to Rynd Farm. Passenger car No. 61 was named for Capt. Andrew B. Funk, who was involved with oil drilling in 1861. (Photograph by Kenneth C. Springirth.)

Northbound Oil Creek and Titusville Railroad train at State Park Road is crossing Oil Creek north of Petroleum Centre station. Car No. 66 is the only operating railway post office in the United States. Built in 1927 for the Chesapeake and Ohio Railroad, it was later sold to the Bangor and Aroostock Railroad. The car, donated to the railroad in 1989, was restored by volunteers. (Photograph by Kenneth C. Springirth.)

South Drake Street in Titusville is about to be crossed by this northbound Oil Creek and Titusville Railroad passenger train to Titusville on October 18, 2009. The open gondola car behind the locomotive is popular for train riders. (Photograph by Kenneth C. Springirth.)

Visit us at
arcadiapublishing.com

....